Fun Is Good

Employee Engagement Consultants

We are passionate about helping organizations develop and sustain a positive, fun and creative culture for their employees and customers alike.

We teach teams and companies of all sizes to adopt an engaging and collaborative culture. We do this through inspiring, fun and actionable keynote speeches, seminars and training sessions delivered by nationally recognized speakers and industry experts.

Website: FunIsGoodTeam.com
Email: Fun@funisgoodteam.com
Phone: 952-334-3030

ANOTHER
BORING,
DERIVATIVE,
PIECE OF CRAP
BUSINESS
BOOK

LAUGH   LEARN   LEAP

ANOTHER BORING, DERIVATIVE, PIECE OF CRAP BUSINESS BOOK

LAUGH   LEARN   LEAP

MAKE THE FIRST BASIC LEAP
IN WORK IN 100 YEARS,
LAUGHING ALL THE WAY

MIKE VEECK & ALLEN FAHDEN

Published by Advantage, Charleston, South Carolina.
Member of Advantage Media Group.

ADVANTAGE is a registered trademark and the Advantage colophon is a trademark of Advantage Media Group, Inc.

Printed in the United States of America.

ISBN: 978-159932-472-2
LCCN: 2014933262

Book design by George Stevens.

This publication is designed to provide accurate and authoritative information in regard to the subject matter covered. It is sold with the understanding that the publisher is not engaged in rendering legal, accounting, or other professional services. If legal advice or other expert assistance is required, the services of a competent professional person should be sought.

Advantage Media Group is proud to be a part of the Tree Neutral® program. Tree Neutral offsets the number of trees consumed in the production and printing of this book by taking proactive steps such as planting trees in direct proportion to the number of trees used to print books. To learn more about Tree Neutral, please visit www.treeneutral.com. To learn more about Advantage's commitment to being a responsible steward of the environment, please visit www.advantagefamily.com/green

Advantage Media Group is a publisher of business, self-improvement, and professional development books and online learning. We help entrepreneurs, business leaders, and professionals share their Stories, Passion, and Knowledge to help others Learn & Grow. Do you have a manuscript or book idea that you would like us to consider for publishing? Please visit advantagefamily.com or call 1.866.775.1696.

For Phil.

TABLE OF CONTENTS

ACKNOWLEDGEMENTS

THIS BOOK IS A 300+ PAGE
THANK YOU NOTE.

We owe the following people greatly for all their support in making *Another Boring, Derivative Piece of Crap Business Book* a reality.

Libby Veeck	*Patti Boysen*
Fran Zeuli	*Margie Albert*
Wendy Zeuli	*Karla Nelson*
Trudi Mendoza	*Don Yoakum*
Jenna Wolf	*Bill Tucker*
George Stevens	*And the maniacs at the*
Adam Witty	*Gold River Starbucks*

A special acknowledgment to Maria West who rewrote the first draft of the book to give it life and zest with her unique turn of a phrase.

INTRODUCTION

Nobody reads the introduction.

CHAPTER 0

DISCO SUCKS:
SO DO BUSINESS
BOOKS

(HOW TO NAVIGATE THIS
ONE-OF-A-KIND BOOK)

 INNOVATION #1
We reinvent the business book to make you laugh.

Since most people only read a single chapter of a business book, we made it easier for you. We condensed the whole book into one chapter. Read it, and you will get the main points of the whole book. Then, the rest of the book gives you 49 chapters of funny stories that illustrate the main points.

You can start with chapter one, or skip around and read the funny chapters first, using the links back to chapter one.

"SEVENTY-FIVE PERCENT OF PEOPLE WHO BUY BUSINESS BOOKS READ ONLY ONE CHAPTER."

—*AMERICAN BOOKSELLERS ASSOCIATION*

Mike Veeck, the man *Rolling Stone* magazine claims killed disco, is out to kill business books. "Disco Sucks" read the signs that fans hung up in 1979 in Comiskey Park. Promotions director Veeck ran ads that screamed, "Bring your disco records to the White Sox game, and we'll blow them up with dynamite in a dumpster." The team usually drew 20,000 people a game. Their stadium held 46,000. That night 90,000 people showed up at the ballpark.

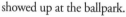

15

As the owner of a string of highly-successful, attention-getting minor league baseball teams, Veeck's funniest and craziest promotion stories make up half of the chapters in this book.

MOTIVATIONAL POSTERS SUCK. SO DO BUSINESS BOOKS.

Allen Fahden, the man *Fortune Magazine* credits for inventing the first *de*motivational posters, is out to change business books. "Give up. You're a loser. No motivational crap is going to change that," reads the first of 49 Suckcess Posters that start the chapters of this book. To implement this and other ideas, he used his own system of the four core work natures: creator, advancer, refiner and executor.

BUSINESS BOOKS SUCK.

That's why we wrote this book. Where business books zig, this book zags.

- We rethought the form.

- We rethought the content.

- We rethought the experience.

Tired of boring, derivative, piece of crap business books? So are we. Too often we've felt suffocated by tedious jargon and long, tiresome processes that seemed meaningless. Because both authors are naturally creative, most people we have known thought we were downright insane for some of our marketing ideas. We share the same core work nature: creator. This means we think like 35 percent of the people who love to generate ideas and innovate. This will demonstrate how to go to all four core work natures at the right phase of the work process to get new ideas implemented three to five times faster, and way better.

BUSINESS BOOKS' FORM USUALLY SUCKS.

The form: Why do 75 percent of those who buy business books read only one chapter? In most busi-

Tired of boring, derivative, piece of crap business books? So are we.

ness books you get just enough new ideas for maybe a magazine article. The rest is filler.

We rethought the form. Now you get the whole book in our Chapter 1. But you can read the fun stories first, if you prefer in Chapters 2-50. If you start with chapter one, you get an overview of the processes that help you create and execute stand-out ideas. If you like a technique, you can refer to another part of the book that illustrates it with a story. If you never read any of the stories, no problem. You've got the gist already.

BUSINESS BOOKS' CONTENT USUALLY SUCKS.

The content: 350,000 books published every year rarely inject many completely new ideas into the business world. This book gives you one of them. Redeal the work so you and others work *in* your strength-based role (who you really are) on content you're passionate about (Why you're motivated to do it.) We call that Peakwork, and it replaces all the Weakwork you're usually forced to do. Start doing that, and most of your brick walls go away.

So, we rethought the content. This book takes you on a ride through some crazy ideas and how they happened. Some were edgy. Most were not politically correct, and some were just plain ridiculous.

THE EXPERIENCE OF MOST BUSINESS BOOKS SUCKS.

Over a decade ago, the best selling business book was Dilbert. It stayed at the top longer than any other business book. Readers felt comfort and camaraderie in shared laughter at the pain and frustration of working in an office. Seeing the ludicrousness of so much of the work world opened their minds to approaching work differently:

- Why do you have to give up content for laughs?

- Why do you have to give up laughs for content?

- When you're bored, you lose your brain's oxygen and go to sleep.

🞘 When you're laughing, you ramp up your brain's oxygen, which gives you the capacity to learn new things.

🞘 When you learn new things, you open up new ways to create what you want.

THE BARRIER TO BEING DIFFERENT
IS HAVING ORIGINAL IDEAS.
BE DIFFERENT OR DIE.

"DIFFERENT ISN'T ALWAYS BETTER,
BUT BETTER IS ALWAYS DIFFERENT."
—*MARSHALL THURBER*

BE A DUMBASS.

"IT'S THE ULTIMATE UNCONTESTED
MARKET SPACE."
—*MIKE VEECK AND ALLEN FAHDEN*

Original ideas go against everything we've ever learned:

▣ Want your parents to treat you well? Be normal.

▣ Want to be popular in school? Fit in with the crowd.

▣ Want to do well in a company? Don't rock the boat.

ALL OF OUR LIVES, WE'VE BEEN TOLD TO FIT IN AND CONFORM.

NOW, SUDDENLY, EVERYBODY WANTS ORIGINAL IDEAS.

HOW DO YOU GET THEM?

In a recent IBM Global Study, 72 percent of 2500 CEOs listed innovation as one of their top three priorities.

In another survey, sponsored by AIGA, 85 percent of employers who hire creative people say they can't find the applicants they seek.

http://www.aiga.org/what-are-employers-looking-for-in-a-creative-professional/

But being different is hard. In fact, despite all the lip service to being innovative, organizations are self-perpetuating and naturally kill anything that differs from the norm. For this reason, an organization is the hardest place to create, launch and implement something different.

Even when you're not stifled by an organization, it's hard to be different. Try searching your idea online (in quotation marks to make it exactly your words in your order) and your idea has already probably had hundreds of thousands, if not millions, of hits. This means not only have others thought of it, they've most likely already implemented it.

SOCIAL MEDIA IS NOT A STRATEGY. SAYING SOMETHING *DIFFERENT* MATTERS MORE THAN WHERE YOU SAY IT.

If you think social media is the answer, so does everyone else. But remember, media is just where you say it, not what you say. When you're saying the same thing as everyone else, you lose the battle for attention. If you use the same old direct marketing tactics online that have been annoying people through snail mail for decades, you will put out a lot of effort and make 90 percent of your audience roll their eyes and click away. Direct marketing using social media is just a new place to say the cheesy, insincere tripe people have always hated.

SEARCH ENGINE OPTIMIZATION MAKES YOU JUST LIKE EVERYONE ELSE.

The paradox: The more people you reach, the less likely you are to stand out. That's because everything you do to get found on search engines makes you the same as everyone else. You have to use key words that people doing a search in your category are using, which means all your competitors most likely use the same key words.

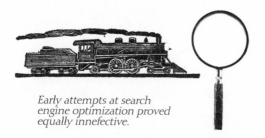

Early attempts at search engine optimization proved equally innefective.

Unless you make a big effort to show up as different in the first page view, you're doomed to be another "me too" offering. Remember, when the choices all look the same, people buy at the lowest price. The only way to compete when you are one of the crowd is by slashing your prices.

As author and speaker Patrick Schwerdtfeger says, "There are 100 million people on Twitter. Are 95 percent of them wasting their time? Absolutely."

 **INNOVATION #2**
We reinvent thinking to create big ideas.

HOW TO BE DIFFERENT: GIVE UP TRYING TO DO SOMETHING SMART. EVERYONE ELSE ALREADY THOUGHT OF IT.

Trying to be smart? Don't bother. It's tough to be smarter than a billion other people who beat you to it. Instead, think of something different and dumb. A Google search will show you how different you are. Let's say you search your smart idea in quotes for exact word order, and the search engine gives you a million links. That means your idea has already been implemented, maybe even a million times.

Smart

Different ....

Same

Dumb

But search a dumb idea and you'll look like a creative genius—seventeen hits, and many of them word combinations that mean something other than your idea.

DO SOMETHING STUPID? INTENTIONALLY? THAT'S JUST...STUPID.

We couldn't be more serious. Sometimes stupid will kill you. But do stupid right, and it's genius.

This boring, piece of crap, derivative business book shows you how to:

- ▣ Get twice your share of revenue by being different

- ▣ Be different by having big ideas

- ▣ Have big ideas by being willing to be stupid

 INNOVATION #3
We reinvent work to get big ideas implemented.

THE BETTER THE IDEA, THE DEADER THE IDEA.

The more unusual your idea, the better chance of a big hit. Sadly, the bigger the idea, the more likely someone will try to kill it when you ask for help. If you can accept and capitalize on the fact that people are different, you can stop beating your head against a wall of opposition, and make life a lot more fun.

Eighty-five percent of people naturally want to kill your idea, for three different reasons. Their instincts keep good ideas from the problems they should be solving. All three types have their own special reasons for wanting to destroy your brainchild:

- Creators, because it's not their idea

- Refiners, because they can see too much wrong with it

- Executors, because it's a threat to the system

PEOPLE ARE DIFFERENT. THEY'RE ALL STARS AT SOMETHING.

Understand what motivates people, and you can route your ideas to the right person at just the right time. This will knock 60–80 percent off how long it takes to get things done.

- Smarten a stupid idea by going to the right person at the right time.

⬚ Implement your big idea in one-third of the time by handing off to the right person at the right phase of the project.

Then, if you want to go deeper and get new things done three to eight times faster, we'll show you ways to:

⬚ Get a starring role map of your people

⬚ Use the three actions to transform to a high performance organization

⬚ Rearrange the work so you hand it off just in time to the right star for the next action

HOW A COUPLE OF NUT JOBS CAN INSPIRE YOU.

Chapters 2 through 50 start with a **laugh** and make a **learning** point. Then they show an action that can allow you to **leap:**

Laugh. The University of Maryland found that laughter gets oxygen to your brain. This greatly boosts creativity and helps you learn.

How a couple of nut jobs can inspire you.

Learn. When you learn new things, you get new ideas. When you get new ideas, you can do new things, which then lets you leap in your life and work.

Leap. But we can all stand to take a leap, especially in an age of confusion and heavy competition.

Each chapter is designed to make you laugh, learn, leap.

This book covers crazy and stupid in four domains, all of which are critical to success in today's crazy and sometimes stupid world.

1. Be daffy (creating big ideas). If you can't think of a smart way to be different, explore the stupid ones. You can win just as big doing something that others won't do. And it's much faster and easier than finding something they can't do.

2. Be a dumbass (choosing big ideas). We'll show you a multitude of doomed ideas. You'll think, "That's not going to end well." But we tried them and they usually did end surprisingly well. But not always in a way we had predicted.

3. Be deft (selling big ideas). Go to the right person at the right phase of the project, and you'll land on your feet every time. An unsold idea is a dead idea. And dead ideas don't help anyone. Learn to start with the creators and the advancers, and finish with the refiners and executors. If the wrong person kills your idea, you don't gain or learn anything.

4. Be done (implementing big ideas). An unfinished project is a dead idea too. Getting it done doesn't mean you have to do it. You just have to go to the right person at the right phase of the project. Certain people are experts at finishing projects. We'll teach you how to change the work to fit the people, rather than always having to change yourself to fit the work.

CHAPTER 1

THIS IS THE CHAPTER THAT GIVES YOU THE CONTENT OF THE WHOLE BOOK.

I f you choose to read Chapter 1 first, you can read some funny stories, afterward, in Chapters 2–50, and learn how the ideas and methods in the book apply in real life. If you have read Chapters 2–50 already, this will help you understand the practical lessons they illustrate. Feel free to jump around. There are links back and forth between chapters.

BY BEING DIFFERENT, DISCO
DEMOLITION BROUGHT 90,000
PEOPLE TO A BALLGAME.
(FOR A FUNNY STORY ON
THIS, SEE CHAPTER 2.)

Today it's more vital than ever to be different, or you die.

"CAPITAL ISN'T SO IMPORTANT IN
BUSINESS. EXPERIENCE ISN'T SO
IMPORTANT. YOU CAN GET BOTH
THESE THINGS. WHAT IS IMPORTANT
IS IDEAS. IF YOU HAVE IDEAS, YOU
HAVE THE MAIN ASSET YOU NEED,
AND THERE ISN'T ANY LIMIT TO WHAT
YOU CAN DO WITH YOUR BUSINESS
AND YOUR LIFE."

—*HARVEY FIRESTONE*

Like sheep to the slaughter, millions of people imitate the
Internet marketing formula. But, ironically, everything you
do to get found by the search engines dooms you to be
the same as everyone else: focusing on keywords, offering

content people are
already looking for,
doing what every-
one in your business
category does makes
you searchable, but not
memorable.

*Like sheep to the slaughter,
millions of people imitate the
Internet marketing formula*

IF YOU ARE THE SAME,
YOU HAVE NO VALUE.

Being the same as your competitors makes you a commod-
ity. And people buy commodities at the lowest possible
price. Your customers, seeing no difference, will choose
whichever option is cheaper. So, unless you take drastic action to be different once they find you, you will usually lose
the price war.

HOW TO BE DIFFERENT AND GET
A HIGHER PRICE: BE WORTH IT.

When you're different, you operate in a category of one.
Nobody can compare you with other apples, because you're

If you're the only orange, you don't have to be the best one to command the highest price.

an orange. And if you're the only orange, you don't have to be the best one to command the highest price. You just need to be who you are, and make sure it demonstrates enough unique value that they want you.

BELIEVE THE RESEARCH: FOURTEEN PERCENT OF COMPANIES GET 61 PERCENT OF PROFITS.

The more crowded it gets, the more different you need to be. The studies show that you win big by being different. Only 14 percent of all companies get a whopping 38 percent of the sales and 61 percent of the profits, according to *Blue Ocean Strategy* by Renee Mauborgne and W. Chan Kim. That means a very small percentage of businesses make most of the money. So what makes them special?

They communicate benefits that everyone else misses. This gives them more appeal than everyone else in the market.

SHOW A UNIQUE BENEFIT THEY CAN BELIEVE IN.

There is a simple formula for how to market in a way that communicates a unique but credible benefit. The result: Show customers three things well and get 240 times the results:

- ▣ dramatic difference

- ▣ overt benefit

- ▣ reason to believe

And dramatic difference made up a huge 55 percent of the 100 percent.

*Source: *Eureka Ranch* founder Doug Hall's analysis of more than 900 marketing journal studies. **To avoid problems, ask the right people "What could go wrong?" Then don't freak out when they tell you. (For a funny story on this, see Chapter 3.)**

"IN EVERY WORK OF GENIUS, WE RECOGNIZE
OUR ONCE REJECTED THOUGHTS."

—*RALPH WALDO EMERSON*

Most of us know plenty of people who seem to kill every different idea that comes along. Why? Because certain people have instincts to protect the system. They automatically look into the future and point out everything that might go wrong. But a creator can take this as trying to destroy their innovation. This usually starts a fight between the person who has the idea, and the one who critiques it.

YOUR JOB: LISTEN TO THEIR FEEDBACK AND AVOID THE FIGHT.

Think of it this way: By failing the idea in concept form, you can get the flaws out of it quickly and cheaply. For his Disco Demolition, if Mike had any notion that 90,000 people were going to show up at the ballpark, he could have hired security for more than 30,000.

Many of your ideas have easily recognizable flaws. You just need to get the right people predicting them in the right atmosphere. Instead of defending your idea from someone who seems to want to kill it, what if you could solve their objections and make the idea even stronger? Start with this rule: Never kill an idea. If it doesn't work today, it could work soon, because everything changes.

DON'T MISS A BRILLIANT IDEA BECAUSE IT HAS ISSUES.

(For a funny story on this, see Chapter 4.)

> "THE ESSENTIAL PART OF CREATIVITY IS NOT BEING AFRAID TO FAIL."
>
> —*EDWIN H. LAND*

Some people see a good idea and run with it. They keep it alive by not showing it to anyone. They push it forward into reality. But on that side of the coin you can get hit by crippling consequences if you take the idea too far before addressing the flaws. That's why we say: **don't be married**

to your idea exactly as it is. It will always change as it hits reality.

So go to the naysayers early and often. If they come up with an issue you can't solve, get some help. If you still can't overcome it, at least your eyes are open to the risks. Sometimes you take them; sometimes you don't.

IF IT SUCKS TO EXCESS, IT'S SUCKCESS.

In the mid-nineties, when we had the idea for the Suckcess posters. They were the first of their kind. One of the posters had a word you couldn't say on TV at the time (see the poster in Chapter 39). The people whom we call the refiners said, "Get rid of that word. It will offend people."

"What do you care?" the advancer pointed out. "You don't have any business anyway." That poster turned out to be our best seller.

When you treat each criticism only as an idea, you get to kill the objection if you solve it. Then the new idea is much stronger than the old one.

HALF THE PEOPLE ARE HUNGRY FOR SOMETHING DIFFERENT

(For a funny story on this, see Chapter 5.)

Researchers created the Diffusion of Innovation over 100 years ago (bell curve graphic). It identifies the different rates at which people adopt change. Heavily researched, this insightful chart has been used extensively to understand consumer product markets. But the concept has never before been used to identify how people accept change at work—until now.

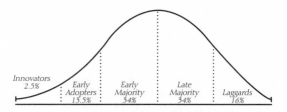

| Innovators 2.5% | Early Adopters 13.5% | Early Majority 34% | Late Majority 34% | Laggards 16% |

Once you understand *adoption nature*, you will realize that there are two kinds of people: those who adopt new things early, and those who adopt new things later.

More than 100 years of studies show that people are different in how they accept change. The attitude to innovation breaks down as:

- ◘ Innovators, 2.5 percent

- ◘ Early adopters, 13.5 percent

- ◘ Early majority, 34 percent This first 50 percent is mostly creators and advancers

- ◘ Late majority, 34 percent

- ◘ Laggards, 16 percent This last 50 percent is mostly refiners and executors

YOU CAN ALSO USE A BAD IDEA FOR ATTENTION AND PUBLICITY. WHAT'S AWFUL TO ONE IS AWESOME TO ANOTHER.

(For a funny story on this, see Chapter 6.)

Sometimes, you don't even have to get the flaws out of a bad idea. You just do it for the following reasons:

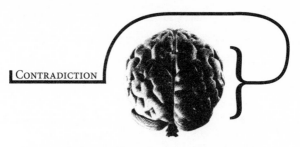

CONTRADICTION

A contradiction forces the viewer into the right brain, because the left brain can't process it.

1. If you purposely propose an idea that at first seems bad, the human mind will try to find good in it. People will at least pay attention and talk about an idea that is different, even if it's questionable. We participated in tests that show that a contradiction forces the viewer into the right brain, because the left brain can't process it. In an era when marketers starve for ways to stand out, this can be very useful.

2. The media loves an irreverent idea. If you get some heat for it, apologize quickly and take responsibility. Many people usually admit that it was funny. Warning: We do live in dangerous times, and there

are some lines you don't want to cross. So test your ideas on people, and if you don't know already what you can't do, you'll learn pretty fast.

BE DIFFERENT AND YOU'LL
ATTRACT THE EARLY ADOPTERS.
THEY LAUNCH MARKET CHANGE.

"ONCE WE RID OURSELVES OF
TRADITIONAL THINKING, WE CAN GET ON
WITH CREATING THE FUTURE."

—JAMES BERTRAND

Thousands of people waited in line for eight hours to get the first iPhone. Why? Because it was different. Yes, it delivered benefits. But it also reflected the cutting edge, change-oriented mindset of the early adopters who clamored to be the first to have one. Early adopters love to do, or have, something before everyone else. "I didn't care that I found out two months later that I had paid $200 too much," Allen explains. "I got 60 extra days with one of the most elegant pieces of technology ever developed."

The hook? When Steve Jobs said, "We didn't do the iPhone to get a share of the phone market. We did it because it was the phone that we all wanted, and it didn't exist."

But the first iPhone didn't take off nearly as fast as the later iPhones and the iPad. That's because 110 years of research shows that the early adopters normalize new things, making

Early adopters normalize new things, making later adopters comfortable enough with the new thing to try it themselves.

later adopters comfortable enough with the new thing to try it themselves. Once consumers in the mainstream market had seen iPhones being used by the public and the media and then recognized that iPhone technology improved with each new generation, they felt safe to adopt this new type of phone for themselves.

WHEN YOU'RE DIFFERENT, PEOPLE NEVER FORGET IT.

(For a perfect example of this, see Chapter 7.)

The Von Restorff Effect shows how elements are remembered when perceived in a sequence.

Researchers found that the best remembered are the first and the last elements. This is why in magazine advertising, you pay for a premium position when you get the back cover or the inside front cover.

Researchers call this primacy and recency.

Primacy: The first element that is seen by the viewer goes into long-term memory and occupies the position for first retrieval.

Recency: The last element stays in short-term memory and is immediately accessible for recall as well.

Therefore, the first and the last elements are the best remembered.

However, Von Restorff also found that if any element in this sequence significantly breaks the pattern, it is remembered far in excess of the first and the last. In a sense, it creates its own category. Find a way to create your own category.

A DIFFERENT WAY TO BE DIFFERENT: HOW TO STOP CREATING AND START COMBINING.

(For a funny story on this, see Chapter 8.)

Everything is already created, Arthur Koestler, in *The Act of Creation*, said. So we don't create, we combine.

Combine the essence of your business with something outside your context.

Great ideas and humor can come from the same principle: The opposite of what we expect.

Stop creating and start combining.

If we combine two elements that have not been together before, they can either fuse into a new truth (aha!), or their absurdity can make us laugh (ha-ha!).

The more dissimilar these elements are, the more powerful the idea. To find the ultimate dissimilarity, go as far as combining two opposites.

START WITH THE OBVIOUS AND DO THE OPPOSITE.

(For a funny story on this, see Chapter 9.)

To create Allen Fahden's one-book bookstore, it took just a few questions. It seems simple, but you must be rigorous with your answers to be sure you get to something really different.

To create Al Fahden's one-book bookstore, it took just a few questions.

Step one: Ask what's obvious about your category. (The best is when you find something so obvious that no one even thinks about it. It's automatic.) The category in this case is books. What's obvious? Sold in bookstores.

Then, sometimes you need to ask another obvious question to get to something useful. Bookstores. What's obvious? Thousands of titles. Barnes & Noble. Getting bigger.

What's the opposite of thousands of titles? One title. So I opened a one-book bookstore in downtown Minneapolis. I stocked thousands of copies of one book—my book—in a 1000-square-foot space.

Once you have your single aspect that's the opposite of the norm, everything else must conform to the standard to make your difference stand out. That's why I included everything I could from a traditional bookstore, from the large downtown space to the liberal return policy.

Every idea spawns hundreds of decisions. Now you can make them consciously without hurting the power of the idea.

APPLE HAS DONE SOME
GREAT COMBINING

If you think about how locked up the cell phone providers had made the market, you could have argued that the iPhone was actually a stupid idea. At the time, cell-phone service providers had a lock on the physical phone part of the business. Why would you attack an industry that was so powerful? Then, all phones were these little flip phones. New business seemed to focus on AT&T and Verizon, selling you different ring tones. No manufacturer was innovating. So if you saw the idea for the iPhone, you could reasonably have told Apple: "Your iPhone doesn't have a chance. No one wants a phone like that. People are happy with the phones they have."

But Apple had already been down that road. The company launched the iPod by convincing the music industry to break decades of history, and sell songs for 99 cents on iTunes. But the phone itself wasn't so much a creation as a combination.

When Apple invented the iPhone, the company combined the phone with the mp3 player. But more importantly, it combined with the GPS and Internet browser so you could find businesses and people by location and then call them or go to their website in one click. The elegance is not in the individual technologies but in how they fit together in an easy-to-use format.

TEST YOUR IDEA ON YOUR TARGET CUSTOMERS. IF THEY LAUGH, YOU MAY HAVE HARNESSED SOMETHING POWERFUL.

(For a funny story on this, see Chapter 10.)

You don't have to be a highly-trained psychologist to know if people like your idea. If they laugh, comment positively or want to know more, you have something.

Test your ideas on your target customers.

If they laugh nervously, fold their arms or give you a blank look, you need to delve for more specific feedback. Ask yourself these questions:

▢ Is this person an early or late adopter? If she is a late adopter and you're introducing something new, you're talking to the wrong person.

▢ Is her issue with the idea one of clarity or taste? If it's clarity, ask her what she understands and then give her more information a bit at a time until she gets it. If it's taste, test a bunch more people until you get an idea of how far you should go. Gary Hamel says you don't have a strategy until you know what part of the market you're willing to give up

FORCE YOUR AUDIENCE INTO THEIR RIGHT BRAIN. IT GETS THEIR ATTENTION, AND MAKES THEM LIKE YOU.

(For a funny story on this, see Chapter 11.)

Another useful outcome of left/right brain research: when viewers have high right brain activity, they like what they

FORCE YOUR AUDIENCE INTO THEIR RIGHT BRAIN. IT GETS THEIR ATTENTION, AND MAKES THEM LIKE YOU.

are seeing more. When Allen Fahden was researching an ad campaign for Levi's jeans, he worked with researchers who hooked up teenagers to EEG machines to record their brainwaves while they looked at ads. Dr. Sidney Weinstein, Editor of *The Journal of Neuroresearch*, was the neuroscientist who correlated high right-brain activity with high likeability for the message. The researchers found that the messages that created the most right-brain responses were the ones based on some kind of contradiction.

HOW TO MAKE AN IMPACT: GET THEM IN THEIR RIGHT BRAINS.

(For a funny story on this, see Chapter 12.)

When the left brain sees a contradiction, it doesn't know how to process it. This forces the right brain to get involved.

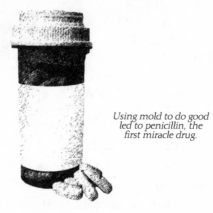

Using mold to do good led to penicillin, the first miracle drug.

Using their right brains makes people happier, so then, they feel more positive about the message. To make a contradiction, often all you need to do is change one word in a true statement to its opposite.

Example: "Mold is bad." Most of us believe that mold is bad, especially if you've ever had water damage at home and had to tear out a few walls.

"THE OPPOSITE OF TRUTH IS NOT NECESSARILY A FALSEHOOD. IT'S OFTEN AN EVEN GREATER TRUTH."

—*NEILS BOHR*

Now change one word to the opposite. "Mold is good." Maybe your first thought says that's a lie. Go beyond that thought and ask this question: How can "mold is good" be true? You can't process that in the left brain. So the contradiction forces you into the right brain.

How can "mold is good" be true? Using mold to do good led to penicillin, the first miracle drug.

WHEN YOU ARE DIFFERENT, NO ONE ELSE CAN COMPETE.

(For a funny story on this, see Chapter 13.)

"THE OPPOSITE OF ANY GIVEN TREND IS WORTH A FORTUNE TO SOMEONE."

—*F. Scott Fitzgerald*

Take the most unquestioned practice in your business and do the opposite. Do you remember the *Seinfeld* episode in which George said he had done everything wrong all of his life? "That would mean if you do everything the opposite of the way you have always done it wrong, then you'd be right," Jerry told his down-and-out friend.

Unlike most of us, George did something about it.

George did the opposite of his instincts and told an attractive woman he was 43 years old, unemployed and lived with his parents. It worked. They started dating. Then he told an interviewer that he had been fired from his last job for sleeping with the cleaning lady. The interviewer hired him on the spot.

Who is your
unbeatable rival?
What's their sword?
What's your gun?

DEFEAT YOUR BEST COMPETITOR
BY CHANGING THE GAME.

(For a funny story on this, see Chapter 14.)

There's always a way to defeat even the best of the best. Do you remember the scene in the first Indiana Jones movie in which Indy runs through the bazaar straight into a man with two swords? As the bad guy whipped and spun the blades menacingly, Jones looked defeated. The crowd gasped, sure that this was the end. Then, Indy nonchalantly pulled out his gun and shot the man. As he put the gun away, while the swordsman lay on the ground, Indy shrugged as if to say, "Well, duh." Who is your unbeatable rival? What's their sword? What's your gun?

YOUR SMART IDEA HAS BEEN DONE A MILLION TIMES? TRY A DUMB IDEA!

(For a funny story on this, see Chapter 15.)

When you have a big idea, the first thing you need to do is Google it. If you get a million hits, it isn't different enough.

But if you have a really dumb idea, Google may reveal that no one has done it. There may be a good reason for that. It's dumb.

How can you make a dumb idea seem like genius?

Unusual ideas affect different people differently:

Idea: "Hey. What if we fill the room with ice cream?"

Reaction 1: feeling. You feel something, but it's just energy.

Reaction 2: unconscious evaluation. The reptilian brain interprets the energy for your protection.

Good feeling: must be a good idea.
Bad feeling: must be a bad idea.

But nothing happens until you attach a thought.

How can you do something that gets almost no hits, makes it relevant to your business and be in a category of one?

Reaction 3: conscious thought. The cerebral cortex weighs why it's a good or bad idea.

Those who feel good about filling the room with ice cream connect the feeling to a pleasure. "Mmm, yes. And it should definitely be Ben and Jerry's fudge brownie."

Those who feel bad connect the feeling to pain. "No. It's going to ruin the carpet."

But this whole set of reactions misses the main point. Imagine how different, fun and newsworthy it would be actually to fill a room with ice cream. I just Googled "fill the room with ice cream" and got only one hit. Then I Googled "fill a room with ice cream" and also got only one hit, albeit a different one. This means almost no one is filling a room with ice cream, or even perhaps thinking about it. How can you do something that gets almost no hits, make it relevant to your business and be in a category of one?

STOP CRITICIZING; START CREDICIZING. ASK: "WHAT CAN GO RIGHT?"
(For a funny story on this, see Chapter 1.)

Have you heard of the law of unintended consequences? It is that no matter how carefully you plan, things will happen that you never foresaw. That could include both good consequences and bad ones. But there is a way to more thoroughly bulletproof an idea for both its downfalls and its potential to bring you benefits.

Start with a stupid idea. Get an early adopter, preferably a creator, to come up with all the ways it could go right. When you credicize (comment by crediting the idea rather than being critical of it), you'd be surprised how many positives can come from a really stupid idea. Then get a refiner to be specific about all the things that could go wrong. But don't let him kill your enthusiasm for your really dumb idea. Next, have the creator come up with ways to fix the potential problems. Do all that, and you have an idea that's so different no one else would do it, and you will have a much better chance of it working.

WHAT RADICAL THINGS ARE YOUR CUSTOMERS CRAVING? JUST ASK!
(For a funny story on this, see Chapter 17.)

If you still can't think of any exciting or even dumb ideas, stop and let it go. Instead, ask your customers what they want and what annoys them about current products. The farther away the new behavior is from what you already do, the more potential it has to be an attention-getting game changer.

Steve Jobs hated asking customers, because he said the customers would tell you they wanted a faster horse and you'd never invent the car. But customers could tell you they wanted a horse they didn't have to feed, that didn't get tired and didn't crap in the road.

Then you could ask, what do eating, getting tired and crapping have in common? They are all things animals do (category). And what's the opposite of an animal? A machine.

NOT ALL FROGS TURN INTO PRINCES OVERNIGHT.
(For a funny story on this, see Chapter 18.)

To find a prince, you have to kiss a lot of frogs. Be sure to have a frog file for all the ideas that seem ugly today. They may shine tomorrow.

To find a prince, you have to kiss a lot of frogs.

Always file all of your ideas, even your worst ideas that everyone hates. Pull them out every now and then, or when there's a big change in the market, and ask yourself how different they still are. Then, if they are still different, credicize them. That means, ask what's right with them. Then criticize. Ask what's wrong with them. If you solve the problems, you might have a winning concept.

Just as people bought lots of food in two of Mike Veeck's most disastrous promotions, (Mime Night and Disco Demolition) the law of unintended consequences can help you as much as it can hurt you.

A SINCERE APOLOGY CAN
GO A LONG WAY. IF THAT
DOESN'T WORK, TELL PEOPLE
YOU'RE GOING TO REHAB.
(For a funny story on this, see Chapter 19.)

Nothing stops a critic faster than not resisting him. Never be afraid to say you were wrong and apologize. In some way you're always part right and part wrong, so it is true.

When you simply admit your wrongdoing or apologize for unintentionally offending people, there's nowhere they can go with it. Apologizing also gets the public on your side, and ready to forgive and move on. After all, everyone makes mistakes.

YOU CAN KILL AN IDEA WITH A LOOK.

(For a funny story on this, see Chapter 20.)

Next time you feel like rolling your eyes at someone's ideas, think of the damage you'll do. Be conscious of your facial expressions and body language. Ideas inspire emotions in

Next time you feel like rolling your eyes at someone's ideas, think of the damage you'll do.

ourselves and others. As soon as we hear an idea, the battle begins. The brain connects the thought to the feeling, bringing up an emotion. If we credicize and primarily see the good in an idea, we feel emotions such as joy, amusement or anticipation. When we criticize and react to what we think is a bad idea, we feel annoyance, disapproval or apprehension. Feelings are strong, and can propel people to take different sides, pushing for change on one side, and fearing disaster on the other side. But you can predict the outcome and take steps to make it a happy ending.

DON'T ELIMINATE COMPETITORS; FIND MORE OF THEM.

(For a funny story on this, see Chapter 21.)

Who or what is your competition in a field related to your immediate business category? How can you take that competition on directly?

We asked ourselves how we could compete for the baseball dollar. Our baseball teams don't compete with other professional teams, except on the field, because the other teams are in other cities. We also don't compete with amateur baseball. Unlike pro ball, attendees often go because of some personal connection with the players. So, when it comes to drawing fans, what is our true competition?

We zoom out, like the lens on a movie camera. It backs us out to a wider shot so we can look at a bigger market. Do we compete for the sports dollar? You might think it would be other sports teams in the market. And while that's true to some extent, other sports such as pro football, basketball, and hockey for the most part play at other times during the year.

Who or what is your competition in a field related to your immediate business category?

Zoom out again. Do we compete for the entertainment dollar? Every game we play takes place at the same time as some other form of entertainment. People choose to go to a baseball game instead of going to something else: game versus movie; game versus restaurant; game versus party.

Zoom out to see your real competition, and imagine a slice of a bigger pie. Opportunity and new business is not always where you expect it to be. In this case, you'd think it would be competitors who do what we do. But it's not. It's competitors who do something different that our customers choose instead. Once you identify these competitors, you can devise market strategies that will divert customers away from them and over to you. A family can choose going to a baseball game where they are entertained and get to interact more with each other, instead of going to the movies.

THE "SAFEST" BUSINESS IS THE HARDEST TO WIN.

(For a funny story on this, see Chapter 22.)

When we have an idea, the reptilian part of the brain—the one that warns us of danger—evaluates whether the idea will cause us harm. Where does that part of the brain look first? It looks for precedent. Has anyone done this before? Is anyone doing it now?

If we find precedent, our idea looks much safer: "This company did it, and they made millions of dollars."

But when someone has already had your idea, it's actually less safe. This means your customers already have an alternative to you. This means they can buy, or have already bought, that alternative at a better price, for better service or for higher quality. In direct competition, someone always loses. If the competitors were there first, you have to do more to get their customers to switch. If you're the same as they are, their customers have no reason to change to you.

IF YOU'RE THE
SAME AS YOUR
COMPETITORS,
WHAT DOES
THAT MAKE YOU?
IRRELEVANT.

What does this make you? Irrelevant. Not the most profitable market position.

YOU CAN BE BLINDSIDED BY A BAD OUTCOME, OR EVEN A GOOD ONE.

(For a funny story on this, see Chapter 23.)

The comedian Steven Wright said, "You can't have everything. Where would you put it?" Well, the same thing is true about knowledge. You can't know everything. The volume of knowledge is increasing too fast, especially in the area of "what you don't know that you don't know."

Every time we embark upon a new idea, we naturally fear what we don't know that can go wrong. So why don't we ever think about what we don't know that can go right? Some people believe that the most negative person in the room is perceived as the smartest. Yes, but that person is also perceived as the most negative. Try

Every time we embark upon a new idea, we naturally fear what we don't know that can go wrong.

doing the opposite. Instead of warning people about what can go wrong, warn them about what could go right. Consider the following angles.

"If you make people laugh, they might like you. And if they like you, they might buy you instead of the competition, which doesn't make them laugh." Some people call that establishing a brand.

"If you go out of your way to help someone or thank someone, that person might tell their friends, or give you a good review." This could actually get you more customers. A single act of kindness could actually do more for you than hours and hours of search engine optimization. Do something different. Do something wonderful. Then get blindsided by a good outcome.

WHEN A SAFE IDEA GOES BAD, IT HURTS MORE.

(For a funny story on this, see Chapter 24.)

When you do everything right (meaning you can prove beforehand it will work, because everything you are doing has been done before), then you have a safe idea. Unfortunately, the belief that it is safe raises expectations. This means, no matter how good your outcome, if it doesn't measure up to what you promised, you've failed. Sales guru Larry Wilson once said, "Pain is the difference between what we expect and what we get."

Which coach keeps the job longer: the one who promises a championship in three years or the one who says, "We just want to get a little better every game"?

HIDE YOUR GOOD POINTS IN THE RIGHT WAY, AND YOUR AUDIENCE WILL FIND THEM FOR YOU.

(For a funny story on this, see Chapter 25.)

I like to start creative presentations by saying, "Don't expect too much," or "We've taken mediocrity to a new level." It's disarming, and will often dissipate some of the cynicism in the room.

I worked with a brilliant market researcher, Srinivasan Namakkal, who advocated actually lowering expectation as a marketing strategy. Since most messages overhype the product, people are disappointed and don't buy again.

We tried the opposite, underhyping, on an apartment community, Arboretum Villages, named after the nearby forest preserve. Our headline was "Our name may be Arboretum Villages, but there's not one mature tree in the whole place."

Instead of large amounts of disappointed people who didn't rent, they got small amounts of people who did. In six months they went from 18 percent to 90 percent full.

Lowering expectations makes you different.

The good points? Buried in the text: "A few features we've been practical enough to build in for you: nearby laundry rooms, etc."

Lowering expectation makes you different.

IF YOU WANT THE RIGHT CUSTOMERS, MAKE THE JOKE ON YOU.

(For a funny story on this, see Chapter 26.)

Admit your weak spots, and drive away the judgmental and hypercritical customers who would have made you nuts anyway.

Customers are different. Some bring you more than their money. They promote your business. They refer you to more customers. They appreciate it when you give them a good deal. It's a symbiotic relationship, because you both get something out of it.

You'll also get customers who do the opposite. They're attracted by how prestigious you look. If you need to pretend you're someone else to get these customers, you should ask if they are really worth getting. They often turn out to be high-maintenance, unappeasable nightmares that drain your resources and anger your employees. Some say, "Fire these customers." We say, be your genuine self, and you won't draw them to you in the first place. Where will they

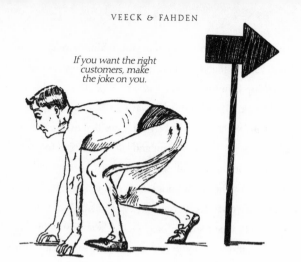

*If you want the right
customers, make
the joke on you.*

go? To your more prestigious competitors. Let them deal
with the headaches.

FIND WHAT'S FUNNY, APPLY IT TO YOUR BUSINESS AND MARKETING, AND YOUR WORLD TRANSFORMS.

(For a funny story on this, see Chapter 27.)

If a thought makes you laugh, hang on to it. It will make
you smarter. A University of Maryland study shows that

laughter brings more oxygen to your brain. Norman Cousins claimed that he conquered a debilitating disease by watching funny movies. (*Anatomy of an Illness*, published by Norton, 1979, 2005) He was in a Moscow hospital in 1964 and was not getting better. He decided to take responsibility for his own treatment and left the hospital to stay in a hotel. He then got all the Marx Brothers films and any other funny movies he could find. This was no easy feat, as the Internet was decades away, there were no video stores or even VHS tapes, and he was in Cold War Russia. He had to find a movie projector and the actual cinema-ready films

The mind can only hold one thought at a time. Why not make it a joyful thought?

in cans. But he did it. Then, he laughed himself back to health. How could this be?

Studies show that laughter creates endorphins, which lower blood pressure and increase pain tolerance. (Social laughter is correlated with an elevated pain threshold.[1])

1 http://rspb.royalsocietypublishing.org/content/279/1731/1161.full).

The mind can only hold one thought at a time. Why not make it be a fun and joyful thought?

TAKE RISKS, BE GRACEFUL AND ASK FOR WHAT YOU WANT.

(For a funny story on this, see Chapter 28.)

When a customer calls with a problem, why is it that so many employees act indifferently? As consumers, we are used to being treated with suspicion. They ask for our account number, security question, PIN number, last four digits of our Social Security number. How refreshing it would be if someone just wanted to help us.

While customer service has improved, many people still expect a negative experience.

According to the Guerilla Group, **17 percent of customers would switch their account to another company if they were asked. And 68 percent of repeat customers switched just because of the indifference of one worker at their current carrier.**

Imagine if you expect a bad experience, what happens when you get a good one?

- 🎲 An employee who actually empathizes with your pain

- 🎲 An admission that it's the company's fault

- 🎲 An assurance that the employee won't stop until it's solved

You can create more good will with a shock of happiness than you can with years of marketing communication.

Mike Veeck showed this by sending handwritten thank-you notes to his season-ticket holders. Shocking. The team, the

> YOU CAN CREATE MORE GOOD WILL WITH A SHOCK OF HAPPINESS THAN YOU CAN WITH YEARS OF MARKETING COMMUNICATION.

Saint Paul Saints, set records by selling out every game of every season for 17 years.

PEOPLE LEARN MORE FROM FAILURES. FAIL MORE; LEARN MORE.

(For a funny story on this, see Chapter 29.)

Sometimes it's hard to remember a compliment someone gave us, but we never forget the painful moments. Maslow says we pay more attention to threats than opportunities. That's why they don't have to build fences around giraffes. They simply dig a shallow trench. Why? Because giraffes have a great fear of falling. When they are born, their mothers drop them from at least four feet up. The pain from that original fall keeps them terrified of it happening again, even as adults.

What's your fear of falling? Is it the same as your fear of failing? Take another look. You haven't failed until you stop getting back up off the mat.

DON'T BE MEAN. BE SILLY.
(For a funny story on this, see Chapter 30.)

"SEVENTY PERCENT OF ALL CUSTOMERS
WOULD SWITCH SUPPLIERS TODAY IF
THEY COULD JUST FIND ONE THEY
PERCEIVED AS BEING MORE FUN."

—TOM PETERS

How's that for an unlikely piece of business research? Being more fun could get you more customers?

Pick the right target and you can get people on your side no matter what.

Look at your competition, direct or indirect. Is the "fun" position taken? We doubt it. If it's available, go for it. It's easy to do, cheap to implement and rewarding to own. The rest of this book, in one chapter, shows you how to get there from where you are based in human nature.

The hardest thing to do in organizations: Implement innovation—of any kind.

The hardest thing to do in organizations: Implement innovation—of any kind.

Is it any wonder it took 100 years for hotels to adopt the curved shower curtain rod?

Simple problem with big pain: Most hotel guests start their day in a tiny shower enclosure. With a straight curtain rod, the curtain follows the lines of the tub, leaving you little space. So, not only do you already feel trapped in closed-in darkness, but when you turn on the water, it creates a vacuum, sucking the cold, wet and clammy plastic shower curtain onto your naked and groggy body like a slimy creature clinging to its victim in a horror movie. It's a lovely way to say, "Good morning from the folks at Marriott."

Simple idea: Curve the curtain rod on the shower away from the wall. This immediately creates up to 50 percent more space inside the shower, with no costly remodeling work. It also places the curtain far enough away from you, so the curtain can't touch your skin. Great idea. So why did it take more than a century to implement? It is probably because organizations instinctively kill new ideas.

THE BEST TEAMS ARE THE MOST DIVERSE. WIN WITH PEOPLE WHO ARE DIFFERENT FROM YOU: CREATORS, ADVANCERS, REFINERS AND EXECUTORS.
(For a funny story on this, see Chapter 31.)

Eighty-five percent of the people will naturally turn down your new idea, for three basic reasons.

- "It's not my idea"—35 percent (creators)

- "Too many things wrong with it"—25 percent (refiners)

- "It will upset my routine"—25 percent (executors)

The best teams are the most diverse.

▣ Only the advancer, 15 percent, will set priorities and launch a great idea.

Otherwise, any time you launch a new idea, you're running uphill through the mud. Here's why: If you try to push change through an organization, the late adopters will instinctively resist it. It's up to early adopters to make it safe for them.

ENTHUSIASTIC
EARLY ADOPTERS
WILL PROJECT
YOU FORWARD
BY LAUNCHING
GOOD IDEAS
INTO ACTION.

We adopt ideas the same way; we adopt products from our core nature.

If instincts for adopting change are such an important obstacle to success, why has no one measured them in workers before? Because, until now, no one acknowledged that how we accept change affects how we work. But it does every day. Watch the people whose armor goes on when something new is introduced. Observe the people who want to change focus and direction every week.

YOU SHOULDN'T FINISH WHAT YOU START.

(For a funny story on this, see Chapter 32.)

> "WE MOVE INTO THE TWENTY-FIRST CENTURY WITH A NINETEENTH CENTURY WORK MODEL."

—*MICHAEL HAMMER*

One hundred percent of work today is designed for 1 percent of the people. It's designed for each worker to finish each project she starts. But only 1 percent of workers (we call them flexors) are good at doing every stage of the work.

This is why a worker often looks terrified when a manager responds to his idea with the encouraging sounding, "It's your idea -- you can run with it." Managers think they are being progressive and supportive. But the person with the creative idea may have no instincts about how to get it done.

FOUR CORE WORK STRENGTHS ARE REQUIRED TO TAKE A PROJECT ALL THE WAY FROM START TO FINISH.

(For a funny story on this, see Chapter 33.)

Only one out of every hundred people has an equal balance of all four types. No wonder people have trouble keeping up. When you assign work, 99 percent of employees will struggle with one or more phases of it, which causes missed deadlines, shoddy work and lots of posturing, blaming and defending.

Well-managed teams outperform individuals when each person focuses on the part of the project they do best. So

Hand off work that doesn't fit with your core work in nature to someone whose core working nature will easily accommodate it.

why not change the order of the work to fit the strength of the individual? Hand off work that doesn't fit with your core work nature to someone whose core work nature will easily accommodate it. You'll get things done three to eight times faster with far fewer do-overs.

SELL YOUR IDEAS *INSIDE* YOUR COMPANY THE SAME WAY YOU SELL THEM TO CUSTOMERS.

(For a funny story on this, see Chapter 34.)

A lot of consultants say that it's simple to implement a new idea in an organization. "You just go to the early adopters first." But they have no idea how to find the early adopters.

Most people go to anyone with their ideas. **Treat your own company like a market.** Your coworkers buy ideas the same way they buy products, which means they have about a 50 percent chance of taking it to a late adopter too early and getting a bad response.

That's because late adopters kill big ideas. A hundred years of research tell us that it's the early adopters who love big ideas. They love big ideas and are soon bored with the current system. So, the more irreverent your idea, the better you'll do with early adopters. That's why some of the greatest successes start as dangerous ideas. Start with the enthusiastic early adopters and they'll project you forward by launching good ideas into action.

The more irreverent your idea, the better you'll do with early adopters.

DON'T LET LATE ADOPTERS KILL YOUR IDEA. GET THEM TO IMPROVE THE IDEA.

(For a funny story on this, see Chapter 35.)

When refiners and executors tell you they don't like your idea, ask them to be specific and then take the specific problems to a creator and ask him to solve it. You'll be surprised how the game can change when you ask a late adopter to be more specific when he objects to your idea.

FAIL EARLIER TO SAVE MONEY AND TIME!

(For a funny story on this, see Chapter 36.)

If you fail your idea in its concept form before you do any prototyping, you never have to throw anything away. That means you don't waste time and money building things that aren't going to work.

So don't get upset and feel defeated if someone takes issue with your ideas. In fact, go to the late adopters to ask them what could go wrong. Identify the barriers early in the process, when they're faster, easier and cheaper to fix. Collect every objection you can and then have your creators come up with new ideas to fix the problems.

Remember, it works best when the starters and finishers are in the room at different times. Otherwise, emotions flare, and arguments will kill the spirit of innovation before you make any progress. And they might even come to blows as creators feel the refiners are raining all over their enthusiasm for the new ideas (see Appendix A, the SPEED Relay Team).

HAVE YOUR EARLY ADOPTERS DRIVING NEW BUSINESS AND INNOVATION, WHILE LATE ADOPTERS RUN THE SYSTEM.

(For a funny story on this, see Chapter 37.)

Get your starters, the creators and advancers, driving innovation and change for new revenue. Keep the refiners and executors overseeing the processes already in place. For every *proposed* action, there is an equal and opposite reaction.

This means you'll find predictable resistance to your ideas. The more different the idea is, the more resistance you'll get. The hope? You'll also find that you can predict which kind of resistance will come from which people. This resistance comes from their core natures, which are also their strengths.

People are different. You show one person a daring idea. She loves it and wants to move it ahead. You show a different

Have your early adopters driving new business and innovation.

person the same idea and he wants to stop it dead. Same idea, different person.

That's why whom you show your idea to and when you show it matters. If you put the right people in the right place at the right time, you greatly improve your chance of getting your idea implemented.

LEARN HOW TO GET ALL OF YOUR PLAYERS WORKING THEIR STRENGTHS IN RHYTHM WITH EACH OTHER.

(For a funny story on this, see Chapter 38.)

You can innovate much faster once you get a tennis match going between the later adopters (refiners and executors) and early adopters (advancers and creators), so they volley

Learn how to get all of your players working their strengths in rhythm with each other.

back and forth between identifying the problems and solving the issues.

The key to making this work is the advancer. Usually, only the advancer gets along well with the creator and the refiner. Think of the advancer as the point guard who passes the ball around to just the right person at the right time. This person fills two roles: the project manager, who has a great strength in setting priorities and the facilitator and an innate sense of when to move on to the next phase.

If you don't have an advancer, don't ask someone with another strength to fill in. It doesn't work. Instead, go borrow an advancer for your meeting. It can take just a few minutes because no one has to be there all of the time, and it's well worth the dramatically better result you'll get with an advancer's instincts helping you.

EIGHTY-FIVE PERCENT OF PEOPLE WANT TO KILL YOUR IDEA. IT'S IN THEIR CORE WORK NATURE.

(For a funny story on this, see Chapter 39.)

You can't get close to measuring adoption instincts and core work nature with personality assessments such as DiSC and Myers-Briggs. While some of the attributes of personality may seem similar, they are not interchangeable. In fact, they measure different parts of a person, and that's why the profiles do not correlate with each other. Personality profiles can be helpful because understanding people's personalities helps you communicate with them and understand how they think and feel. Core work nature, on the other hand, tells you what phases of work each person can do, such as planning, implementing or completing.

CORE WORK NATURE TRIPLES WHAT GETS DONE BY ORCHESTRATING HANDOFFS TO THE RIGHT PERSON AT JUST THE RIGHT PHASE OF THE PROJECT.

(For a funny story on this, see Chapter 40.)

When you have a novel idea, give it to the advancer, who will connect it to the people and the steps to make it happen.

Who to go to for CPR (concept, plan, reality).

If you have a big idea and want to move it ahead, go to an advancer. An advancer will set priorities and make a plan to implement your big idea.

Also, consult an advancer if you have several ideas and don't know which one will work best. She'll choose the best one in less than a minute.

Core work nature triples what gets done by orchestrating handoffs to the right person at just the right phase of the project.

An advancer is an early adopter with a bent for action. She can see your idea and the sequence of events it will take to get it done. Her input is concepts; her output is plans.

If you have a problem, and you need solutions, go to a creator.

A creator is the other early adopter who likes to shake things up with his ideas.

If you already have an idea, the creator may not buy in because he likes his ideas better.

A creator is an early adopter who tends to think about new ideas rather than an action plan or keeping systems running. He can see your problem in a different way and come up with novel solutions.

REFINERS AND EXECUTORS
WILL MAKE YOUR IDEA BETTER.
JUST ASK THEM TO FORESEE
SPECIFIC PROBLEMS WITH YOUR
IDEA THAT CAN BE SOLVED.

(For a funny story on this, see Chapter 41.)

If you have a plan and you need to find out what can go wrong, go to the refiners and executors.

If you already have a plan and want to implement it, the refiners and executors also won't buy in. They'll tell you it has too much wrong with it. They'll even ask you for more detail, so they can pick it apart.

Refiners and executors are late adopters. Refiners analyze and think. Executors take methodical action. They can see the flaws in your ideas and your plans and can give you some problems to solve. They often think the problems they raise are enough to kill the idea. Yet, they don't realize how easily creators can create concepts to overcome these problems.

IT AIN'T OVER UNTIL YOU'VE TAKEN THE STUPID IDEAS SERIOUSLY.

(For a funny story on this, see Chapter 42.)

Too many meetings suck the will to live out of the room with exchanges like this:

> **Starter:** Here's my idea for a 50-state launch.
>
> **Finisher:** You can't do that. It's illegal in 18 states.
>
> **Starter:** Hey, you don't like my idea; you don't like me.
>
> **Finisher:** I was just saying…

It ain't over until you've taken the stupid ideas seriously.

No one knows it yet, but the meeting is over. People shut down. They say only safe things that they know won't be criticized. The ideas get duller and duller. Nothing happens.

Instead, try it this way:

> **Starter:** Here's my idea for a 50-state launch.
>
> **Finisher:** You can't do that. It's illegal in 18 states.
>
> **Starter:** Thanks for the heads up. What else can go wrong?

DON'T EVER LET SOMEONE'S OBJECTION TO AN IDEA DEFEAT YOU. THERE IS ALWAYS A WAY TO MAKE IT WORK.

(After you collect all the objections, you excuse the finishers from the meeting. If they're not in the room, they won't feel the need to defend their position once someone begins to solve the objection.)

Who's got an idea? How can we fix that?

> **Starter 2:** Well, that means it's legal in 32 states.

> **Starter 3:** We can launch in the 32 states, get a good track record and then lobby in the other 18 to change the law.

> **Starter:** Great idea. What else could go wrong?

DON'T EVER LET SOMEONE'S OBJECTION TO AN IDEA DEFEAT YOU. THERE IS ALWAYS A WAY TO MAKE IT WORK. ASK YOUR CREATORS FOR SOLUTIONS UNTIL YOU FIND OUT HOW.

(For a funny story on this, see Chapter 43.)

Creators look at the world in a different way. Statistically, most of us lose 90 percent of our creativity between the ages of five and seven, when we go to school and learn to follow the rules and narrow ideas of what is important.

Creators are the people who still naturally break the rules. Deep down, many creators still have the open mind of a five-year-old. This means you can go to them expecting one thing, and get quite another. Often, it's a completely novel solution. This can be good if you're stuck, because creators can free you in seconds by approaching the problem from a different context.

A CREATOR WILL KILL YOUR IDEA FOR ONE REASON: IT'S NOT HERS. INSTEAD, GO TO THE CREATOR TO SOLVE THE PROBLEMS WITH THE IDEAS THAT THE LATE ADOPTERS RAISED.

(For a funny story on this, see Chapter 44.)

If you have an idea you love, don't show it to a creator. The better the idea is, the more the creator may want to kill it and replace it with her own idea. Why? If your idea solves a big problem, she'll want it to be her idea that solves that problem. The bigger the problem, the more she wants it.

A creator will kill your idea for one reason: it's not hers.

This means she will probably fight your idea. You'll just lose ground.

Instead, use a creator when you don't yet have an idea, or use a creator to solve objections to the idea you have. That way, by solving a problem with the idea, the creator can imprint your idea with her work, making it partially her own.

YOU DON'T HAVE TO HIRE A TEAM. JUST TAKE YOUR IDEA TO THE RIGHT STRENGTH AT THE RIGHT TIME, TRADE FAVORS AND SOLVE IT IN MINUTES.
(For a funny story on this, see Chapter 45.)

Once you learn the SPEED Relay Team in Appendix A, you don't need to limit it just to meetings. One leading Internet company, often called the most innovative in the world, uses it every day without meetings. They do this by walking around. Once you know who is who, you can save time, money and aggravation by going to just the right person with just the right request. Even if work still requires you to finish what you started, you can still get lots of help along the way.

Why do this? You save so much time you might even have time to have a life. Think of it this way: Just because your workload is 50 percent peak work and 50 percent weak work, that's not how you allocate your time. Since weak work takes you so much longer, it's more like 10 percent peak work and 90 percent weak work. And what does that do to your life? You end the day drained and never get where you want to be.

BE CAREFUL ABOUT WHO WORKS TOGETHER AND WHO DOESN'T.

(For a funny story on this, see Chapter 46.)

Once you have your team together by strengths, you also need to know who not to go to. Just as a handoff to the right person can ramp up your speed and satisfaction, a handoff to the wrong person can stop you dead and even kill your idea or project.

Even though we need every kind of worker, some of us clash easily because of our divergent sensibilities. Natural starters versus natural finishers make up the biggest area of conflict. Here are the best and worst handoffs:

- Good: creator with advancer, refiner with executor

- Bad: creator with refiner, advancer with executor

- Neutral: advancer and refiner

- Other planets: creator and executor

BEFRIEND AS MANY ADVANCERS AS YOU CAN. THEY GET STUFF *DONE!*
(For a funny story on this, see Chapter 47.)

If you do nothing else as a result of this book, find as many advancers as you can. Advancers make all the difference in getting a great idea all the way from start to finish. Advancers will set priorities and launch your best ideas. Without advancers, the great ideas die.

Befriend as many advancers as you can. They get stuff done!

Stop paddling upstream. Don't take an idea to a late adopter. Take it to an early adopter. But how do you find that person?

Map your organization. Once you find out who has which strengths in your organization, you can do several things with it:

1. You can color-code your organization chart by the strengths of the people in each position *(fig. a)*. This will tell you how difficult or easy each function in your business will be, especially with new projects.

Fig. A

ORGANIZATIONAL CHART

C Creator   R Refiner
A Advancer   E Executor

Vice President
C

Group Leader CA   Group Leader R   Group Leader RC   Group Leader ER   Group Leader RE

2. You can slice it the other way and see on a scatter diagram where your people stand on the strength matrix *(fig. b)*. This will tell you how much of each strength you have and where you're missing necessary talents.

Fig. B

TOP 20% OF SALES TEAM

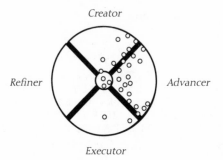

Creator

Refiner   *Advancer*

Executor

3. You can use your knowledge to make midcourse corrections:

   a. Recruit teams that have enough diversity of strengths to succeed.

b. Get buy-in by going to the natural starters (early adopters) first, now that you know who they are. The starters will then make it safe for the natural finishers (later adopters) to buy in.

c. When you want to get something done, go to the natural thinkers.

d. When you want ideas or critiques, go to the natural doers.

WORK SRP: LET YOUR STRENGTH DETERMINE YOUR ROLE AND THEN APPLY IT TO CONTENT THAT AROUSES YOUR PASSION. THAT MAKES YOU A STARRING ROLE PERFORMER.

(For a funny story on this, see Chapter 48.)

All too often people choose their career and life's work on the basis of content that interests them or inspires their passion. If you do that, you're still missing half the picture, which means you can get into a job "doing what you love" and still hate it.

Take Allen's experience, for example:

> I'm passionate about baseball and I hate banks. On the
> strength scale, I'm great at coming up with ideas, and
> I'm weak at doing the detail work. So, the worst place
> I can be is in an area of **low strength, low passion**—
> that's **the lower left hand corner**—so in my case that
> would be in the accounting department, doing the de-
> tail work at a bank. I would hate what I was doing. I
> would be bad at it.

If you go up to the **upper left of the diagram**, I would be in **high strength, low passion**. Imagine a bank hiring me to come up with ideas. This actually happened.

I loved the fact that the bank implemented almost every idea I had. But I developed a bad attitude, because I have no passion for the banking business. Soon, after every victory, I would celebrate but then walk out muttering, "We did all this just to sell another checking account? What the hell's wrong with me?"

HIGH PASSION

LOW STRENGTH

Struggler

Performer

HIGH STRENGTH

Dead Weight

Misfit

LOW PASSION

For the opposite, go down to the lower right of the diagram, to **low strength, high passion**. I love baseball. Imagine if I went to work for a team, but the boss said, "You've got to pay your dues like everyone else, so we're going to start you out processing invoices. You're going to be a payables clerk now for the next year and a half." I would have to tell him, "If you have me doing payables or accounting of any kind, the team will be out of business in two weeks."

Low strength, high passion means you really want to do well, but you struggle. You have a good attitude and bad performance.

In the one we just talked about—**high strength, low passion**—you have a good performance but a bad attitude.

So the ideal place is the upper right of the diagram—**high strength, high passion**—to use your strengths on something you're highly passionate about. Then you've got great attitude and you've got great performance. Those go hand in hand, and it's not just a linear thing; it's more of a geometric progression. Put those together and they're not twice as good—they're six, seven, eight, even ten times as good.

What's inside me that I need to express? Strengths.

What's outside me that gives me purpose? Passion.

STRENGTH OR PASSION? WE NEED BOTH. BE TRUE TO YOUR CORE WORK NATURE AND WORK ON YOUR PASSION.

(For a funny story on this, see Chapter 49.)

I knew a guy who made lots of money and hated to fill out an expense report. Knowing that he traveled a lot, I asked him who did his expense report. "No one," he said, "I eat them."

That's how much he hated expense reports—$70,000 worth.

Soon after, I went to work half-time for an Internet startup. Hating expense reports but not having $70K to burn, the first thing I did was find a detail guy named Kevin. Why? So he could fill out my expense report.

STRENGTH OR PASSION? WE NEED BOTH. BE TRUE TO YOUR CORE WORK NATURE AND WORK ON YOUR PASSION.

When I asked him to, he laughed and said, "Why should I?"

I asked him how long his expense report took him to fill out.

"Fifteen minutes," he said.

"Well, it takes me four hours and I get it back from accounting five times. You do my expenses, and we save the company three hours and 45 minutes."

"Yeah, but what's in it for me?" he shot back, folding his arms.

"What do you need?" I asked.

"I have problems with trade-show setup. I hate them."

"Next time call me," I told him. "I'll give you 10 ideas in five minutes."

"Okay. I'll try it once. We'll see."

Two weeks after Kevin did my first expense report, the phone rang. "Payback time," Kevin said. "I'm at the trade show and almost everyone's here. The CEO, the board, my boss, 10,000 prospects. The only two people who aren't here? The guys who deliver the booth. The booth is not here and is not coming, and the show starts in two hours!

"Do you have anything?" I asked.

"I have the computer so I can demo the website. But everybody else has booths, brochures, lights and dancing girls. I've got 10 by 20 feet of bare concrete floor, and I'm in a fetal position right in the middle of it. You gotta save me."

"You're in Miami," I talked as I thought. "You're near a beach. Do you have a car?"

"Yes."

"Okay. Drive to a drugstore and get some giant plastic trash bags. Go to the beach and fill them with anything you can find that says, "beach": driftwood, shells, palm leaves, pails, shovels, a beach towel. Fill the rest of the bags with sand. Go back and spread the sand over your 10 by 20-foot space at the trade show. Put the other beach items on the sand with the computer open to the company logo. Then, with your finger, write the company's name in the sand, along with the words—so simple it's like a day at the beach."

He told me afterwards that it was the most successful trade show his company had ever had.

He was a brilliant, methodical, detail person who could do an expense report in mere minutes, but coming up with creative ideas on the spur of the moment felt impossible to him. I was an expense report moron, but I could come up with innovative presentation ideas all day long. Symbiosis.

MAKE FRIENDS WITH PEOPLE WHO CAN'T DO SOMETHING FOR YOU. WHEN YOU DON'T EXPECT ANYTHING, YOU'LL NEVER BE DISAPPOINTED.

(For a funny story on this, see Chapter 50.)

You'd be surprised at all the things you don't know about the people you meet. People are just like ideas: All the great ones have something wrong with them. And all the not-so-great ones have a lot more right with them than you'd think.

In our culture we always think that people with the means to help us will. Yet, many times, our biggest benefits come from the people who don't seem to have the means to help us.

When you're launching a business, strategy author Gary Hamel says, "Too much money makes you stupid." So what can help you more than money? How about something customers want, something they can't get from anyone else?

Instead of money, why not get ideas that make you different, and people who can do your weak work from their strength.

And imagine that you do all of it, and stay with it, because you're passionate about what you're doing, and it's way too much fun to stop.

Make friends with people who can't do something for you. When you don't expect anything, you'll never be disappointed.

If you're a creator, get to know as many advancers as possible. Imagine how good it feels when someone who values what you value also likes your ideas.

If you're an advancer, get to know as many creators as possible. Not only will they give you a steady flow of ideas, some of which you can launch, but they will also appreciate you more than almost anyone else in your life will appreciate you.

If you're a refiner, get to know as many executors as possible. Once you think of what needs to be done to make the system even more effective, they will do the details for you without feeling like killing themselves.

If you're an executor, get to know as many refiners as possible. They will protect you from all the other people who want to rush into ideas that haven't been thought through and could disrupt the system.

If you bring more people into your life whose core nature fits your core nature, every moment can be a lot more pleasant and productive. The rest is handoffs.

STAND OUT BY BEING DIFFERENT.
CREATE THESE UNIQUE
OFFERINGS BY USING YOUR SAME
TEAM MORE EFFECTIVELY.

"IN ORDER TO BE IRREPLACEABLE, ONE MUST
ALWAYS BE DIFFERENT."

—COCO CHANEL

If you want to stand out in a world where sameness is encouraged and often required, you need to be different in a way that will benefit or at least appeal to your potential

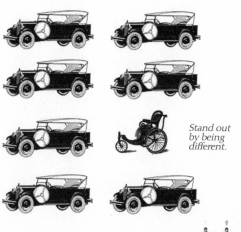

Stand out by being different.

market. To be different, you can combine two opposites or combine a different kind of product or service with your offering the way that Apple combined the phone, the GPS and mp3 player with Internet access.

But at least half of the workers in most organizations fear change and want to kill it. Identify the core work nature of each member of your team, and you can use their talents at the right phase of a project to think up, plan, bulletproof and execute ideas that will make you stand out in increasingly competitive markets. You'll work in your strengths on your passion.

CHAPTER 2

GIVE UP

YOU'RE A LOSER—NO BOOK'S GOING TO CHANGE THAT

THINK ONE PERSON CAN'T MAKE A DIFFERENCE? I KILLED DISCO

BY MIKE VEECK

I hate disco. In 1979 I wasn't alone. Anti-disco backlash was growing. I figured why not capitalize on the increasing antagonism toward fluffy, overproduced music and shiny clothing? And it could help the Chicago White Sox, my employer, and the team my father, Bill Veeck, owned. I enlisted the help of notoriously anti-disco Chicago DJ Steve Dahl. I ran this ad in the paper: "Bring your disco records to Comiskey Park, and we'll blow them up with dynamite."

Raised by a father whose outlandish, groundbreaking promotions eventually landed him in the Baseball Hall of Fame, I knew great ideas could build a career. I was proud of this silly promotion that captured a popular, but untapped sentiment. Disco Demolition was edgy, funny and newsworthy. In a year when the Sox drew 20,000 fans a night, I figured we could draw in as many as 35,000 people to the ballpark with our anti-disco message.

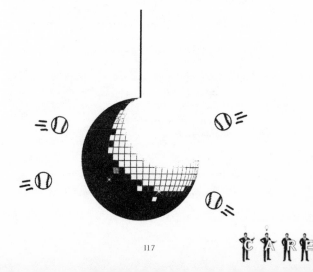

I was wrong.

Over 90,000 disco haters showed up. Unfortunately, Comiskey Park only held 46,000 people. We probably crammed 60,000 into the park that night with standing room only. Unfortunately, I had only hired enough security to handle 35,000.

GIVE UP
DOING THIS

Following the crowd. (The crowd loved disco at its height.) When you follow the crowd, you'll never draw a crowd.

DO THIS INSTEAD

Think about how much you hate the popular trend and attack it. Every trend has a backlash of early adopters waiting for someone to voice their frustration.

Just by being different, the anti-disco night got an amazing 90,000 people to a ballgame.

CHAPTER 3

SUCKCESS
WHEN IT SUCKS TO EXCESS, IT'S SUCKCESS

THEN DISCO
DEMOLITION
KILLED ME

BY MIKE VEECK

On July 12, 1979, at game time, the freeway was backed up for miles with cars we didn't have room for in the stadium parking lot. Donna Summer and Bee Gees records, launched with malicious glee, sailed like Frisbees across four lanes of traffic and then fell to litter the road. Stoners climbed the fences of the park. The scent of weed lay heavy in the air.

I overcalculated how much dynamite we would need to blow up the records of attendees. As combat-fatigue-clad

The explosives blew a crater in the outfield.

DJ Dahl spurred the crowd in a chant of "Disco sucks!" the explosives blew a crater in the outfield. In the aftermath, what Wikipedia now describes as a "small fire" smoldered in the ruins of the field.

The White Sox had to forfeit the second game of the double header. It was only the fourth time in major-league history that a game had to be called due to a failed promotion. It was the last time an American league game was forfeited.

Sometimes a great idea seems like a bad idea at first.

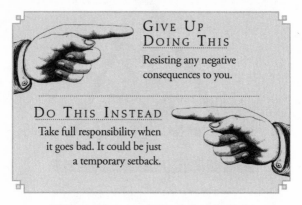

GIVE UP
DOING THIS

Resisting any negative
consequences to you.

DO THIS INSTEAD

Take full responsibility when
it goes bad. It could be just
a temporary setback.

*If Mike had known in 1979 what's in this book,
he would have gone to the right people early and asked, "What could go wrong?"*

CHAPTER 4

ATTITUDE IS ALL
NO ONE WILL NOTICE YOU'RE NOT WORKING

I Rose from the Ashes of the Disco Records

by Mike Veeck

Sometimes a great idea can seem like a bad idea for a really long time. I was blacklisted from major league baseball for ten years.

Eventually, my infamy turned into notoriety. One day, some ten years after the end of my first baseball career, I was finally granted a reprieve. VH1 aired a *Rolling Stone* magazine special on the history of rock and roll. My idea, an idea my father, infamous for his crazy ideas, deemed one of the worst ideas of all time, was declared the event that marked the end of the disco era.

I was finally somebody. I was the destroyer of disco.

I could work with notoriety. I headed back to baseball with a new purpose: to create a fun place for people to enjoy themselves, no matter who won the game.

I rose from the ashes of Disco Records.

125

Give up doing this: being afraid to do something wrong, especially publicly.

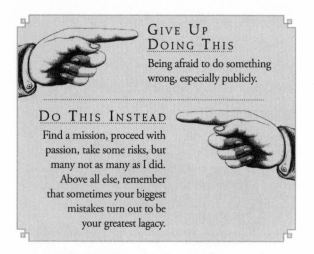

GIVE UP DOING THIS

Being afraid to do something wrong, especially publicly.

DO THIS INSTEAD

Find a mission, proceed with passion, take some risks, but many not as many as I did. Above all else, remember that sometimes your biggest mistakes turn out to be your greatest lagacy.

If you focus only on a concept's weaknesses, you miss the great idea. But if you see only the good, you can get whacked. This book shows you another way. Keep the great idea, but find the people what can show you what flaws to fix.

CHAPTER 5

MOMENTUM

WHEN CIRCLING THE DRAIN, YOU SPIN FASTER AT THE BOTTOM

"We're Number Three, and We Don't Try at All"

by Allen Fahden

What do you do if you're the lowliest player in your category? Take your biggest disadvantage and make it into an advantage. The smallest bank in Bemidji, Minnesota, came to my ad agency to change its image, or at least create some awareness—any awareness—that it existed. Its standing among the other banks in town? It had the least money, the worst location and held a clear position as a solid number three in a three-bank market.

Just the kind of challenge I love.

Don't fight your weaknesses. Embrace them.

We launched the campaign for the Bemidget (Bemidji's midget), the smallest bank with the least money. While other banks bragged about offering more interest, we pointed out that we were the only bank located directly above the La- dies' Municipal Restroom. "How's that for real bank- ing convenience?" We also pointed out that since the family who owned the bank was of Swiss heritage, patrons of the Bemidget had bragging rights to tell people they had their own Swiss bank account.

Don't fight your weaknesses. Embrace them.

Business doubled within two years.

GIVE UP DOING THIS

When people have nothing meaningful to say, they often turn to clichés and platitudes. And potential customers immediately tune out.

DO THIS INSTEAD

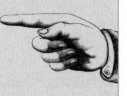

If your advantages over the competition don't mean too much, or if you don't have any advantages, start hawking your disadvantages. The fact that you admit them gives you a refreshing amount of credibility. This opens people up to accepting the advantages you do have and making an emotional commitment to you.

Emotions drive behavior. Fifty percent of people, the early adopters, like to break or reframe the rules. Be different and they'll love it.

CHAPTER 6

PERSEVERANCE
IF YOU PERFORM JUST BADLY ENOUGH, YOU'LL
GET A BIGGER SEVERANCE CHECK

131

VASECTOMY: THE
GIFT THAT KEEPS
ON GIVING

BY MIKE VEECK

You can get great media coverage just by showing poor judgment. As we expected, only two hours after announcing the Charleston Riverdogs would give away one free vasectomy for Father's Day, the wrath of the Catholic Church rained down upon us—and I'm a Catholic. Having to cancel the promotion *was* the media story. Of the torrents of national press about our gaffe, our favorite headline came from the Anchorage *Daily News*: "Promotion Snipped."

133

Write down one idea you snipped. Reconsider it. If the backlash won't kill you, try it. You could come out way ahead. What's your version of Vasectomy Night?

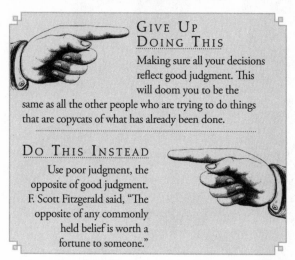

GIVE UP DOING THIS

Making sure all your decisions reflect good judgment. This will doom you to be the same as all the other people who are trying to do things that are copycats of what has already been done.

DO THIS INSTEAD

Use poor judgment, the opposite of good judgment. F. Scott Fitzgerald said, "The opposite of any commonly held belief is worth a fortune to someone."

And don't forget you can also run with a bad idea just for the negative publicity. What's awful to one person is awesome to another.

CHAPTER 7

PRIORITIES
NUMBER ONE: YOUR BUTT

IF YOU'RE
WORRIED ABOUT
COVERING YOUR
ASS, LEARN TO
WALK BACKWARD

BY ALLEN FAHDEN

If you walk backward, you can watch your ass and where you're going at the same time. Now that's a leader.

At age 25 I started an advertising agency. People told me to name it Fahden and Associates. That would be dignified and in the box. I'm not an in-the-box guy. I named it Fahden As In Cat. It was different and I thought it would solve my lifelong problem of people mispronouncing my last name. I've gotten everything from Fayden, Feeden, Fudden, Fawden, and Fooden. Now they could use *cat* as a rhyme. *F* as in *Frank* and *a* as in *cat*.

Fahden As In Cat. It didn't work. People still said: "Fayden as in cat and Fudden as in cat." But then, one day, I realized the best reason that I chose that name. My aunt from Chicago had called the phone company to get my number. "Allen Fahden? Oh, you mean Fahden as in cat?" said the operator. It taught me two things about dumb ideas:

1. If it's different enough, no one will forget it.

2. If you risk alienating uptight people, you can spend your time with fun clients who appreciate your unique attitude.

Stop covering your ass.
Cover your customer's ass.

Strategy guru Gary Hamel says, "Until you know what ground you're willing to give up, you don't have a strategy." Well, I was willing to give up all the uptight clients. If you're fun enough to do businesses with an ad agency called Fahden As In Cat, you're also fun enough to use my edgy ideas in your advertising. Thanks to my silly name, all the ass-coverers were forewarned and stayed away. With enthusiastic clients who had a sense of humor, we won lots of awards.

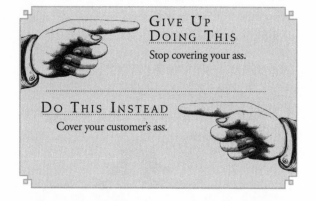

GIVE UP DOING THIS
Stop covering your ass.

DO THIS INSTEAD
Cover your customer's ass.

Do something very different and you'll attract the early adopters first. They thirst for the unique and always start the change.

CHAPTER 8

OPTIMISM
WORRYING THAT YOU'RE OVERQUALIFIED FOR THE BOSS'S JOB

CARE

THE JOYS OF
WINE SLOBBERY

BY ALLEN FAHDEN

If you want to build people's awareness of you, do something that no one will ever forget and everyone will want to talk about. Because wine snobbery was a big trend in my circle, I decided to do an unforgettable wine tasting for clients and friends.

I had everything the finest wine tasting would include:

1. I held it at one of the finest restaurants in town.

2. I booked a private room with a staff of waiters in tuxes. Yes, I had them instruct the group on the five factors necessary for scoring the finest wines.

Just one difference: Instead of trying to be a wine snob, I became a wine slob.

The presentation was pure snobbery and elegance. The product, on the other hand…

With a flourish, the owner introduced the three wines we presented. They were the absolute worst wines of the day: Boone's Farm, Annie Greensprings and Mogen David (Mad Dog 20/20). Between the wines, instead of French bread and brie to clear the palate, they served Wonder Bread, Premium Saltines and Cheese Whiz. My clients and friends loved the party and it was the talk of

If you want to build people's awareness of you, do something that no one will ever forget and everyone will want to talk about.

ad agency circles. One of my friends who owned one of the big ad agencies in town stole the idea for a client party of his own. For years, I had people come up to me saying they had heard about that party and wished I had invited them or wished they had known me at the time because they would have come.

Twenty years later I dined in the same restaurant. A bottle of Mad Dog 20/20 was brought to the table. "Compliments of the owner," our waiter announced. The previous owner's son was now the proprietor. At the time of the wine slob tasting, he was in high school, working in the kitchen. He not only remembered, but had someone run out for a bottle of Mad Dog 20/20 just so it could be delivered to my table.

Build your confidence. Get people to remember you for 20 years. I used to speak at copywriting classes at the local university and deliver the most unforgettable presentation I could think of. I told them the truth about how little viewers remember ads, or even what brand the ad is for. That, among other things, allowed me to work my marketing plan: "Answer the phone when it rings."

Whenever new clients called, usually directors or VPs of marketing, I'd ask them how they had found me. Time and time again they said, "You spoke to my copywriting class 15 years ago."

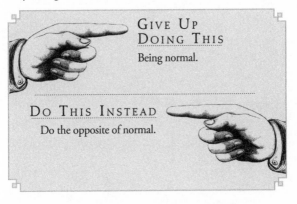

GIVE UP
DOING THIS
Being normal.

DO THIS INSTEAD
Do the opposite of normal.

When you're different, people never forget it. The Von Restorff effect shows anything that breaks the pattern is remembered far better than anything else. (Von Restorff studied memory on elements within a sequence and found people best remembered the first and last element. But then, when he tested any element that broke the pattern in the sequence, it outperformed the first and last.)

CHAPTER 9

QUALITY
DO SOMETHING STUPID, BUT DO IT VERY, VERY WELL

A BLINDING
FLASH OF DUH

BY ALLEN FAHDEN

I've always felt oppressed by the tedious way authors follow the same, boring and predictable marketing rules to promote their books. I wrote a book about using the opposite of what you are expected to do as a way to come up with creative ideas for marketing. One day, as I tried to figure out an innovative way to market my book *Innovation on Demand*, I had a revelation: "What if I used the methods in the book to market the book?"

How's that for original?

Step one: identify what's most obvious.
Step two: do the opposite.

Step one: identify what's most obvious.
Step two: do the opposite.

"What's the obvious way to sell books?" I asked myself. I thought of bookstores—this came before the dominance of Amazon. Bookstores were getting bigger and had thousands of titles. But I had only one book. So I made that my opposite. The ReadDundant Bookstore was born—with thousands of copies of one book, my book, filling 1,000 square feet of retail space in downtown Minneapolis.

To make the idea funnier, and at the same time more powerful, I made the store look like a normal bookstore in almost every other way. I put thousands of copies of my book, only my book, in 13 different departments: Art, Anthropology, Religion, Self-Help, Travel, and so on. I had a book of the month club, my book 12 times a year. I had a top 10 ReadDundant bestsellers list. My book occupied all ten positions on the list. I posted a liberal return policy:

IF YOU'RE NOT COMPLETELY
SATISFIED WITH YOUR BOOK,

IT WILL BE CHEERFULLY EXCHANGED
FOR ANY OTHER BOOK
IN THE WHOLE STORE, YOUR CHOICE.

I didn't make one phone call or issue one press release, but momentum began within a week. I appeared in a local weekly business newspaper, then in newspapers and on radio stations around the country, and then on ABC national news and a BBC special on American culture. A year later, my face beamed out from inside my bookstore in the pages of *People Magazine*. Next to me hung the store's warning to potential thieves: "Shoplifters Welcome." I figured shoplifters had feelings too.

On the strength of the idea alone, this one book bookstore got me in front of 50 million people, and my speaking business took off, too. Can't come up with a good idea? Think of what everyone else is doing. Now think of the opposite and do it.

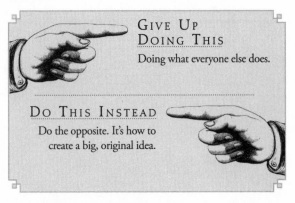

GIVE UP
DOING THIS
Doing what everyone else does.

DO THIS INSTEAD
Do the opposite. It's how to
create a big, original idea.

Once you can solve your idea's problems in the concept phase, you can safely implement a big idea. How? Start with the obvious and do the opposite.

CHAPTER 10

CHERISH TODAY

TOMORROW YOUR JOB IS TOAST

WHAT I LEARNED
FROM THE US
SENATOR WITH THE
"WIDE STANCE"

BY MIKE VEECK

Bobble-head dolls have been done to death by base-ball team promoters across the country. I like to be different. To celebrate National Tap Dance Day, we commemorated the arrest of a good senator from Idaho for tapping his foot in a stall of the Minneapolis-Saint Paul Airport men's room, allegedly to solicit sex. We did this by giving away a toy replica of a toilet stall, with a bobbing foot sticking out. The world's first bobble-*foot* doll.

You want ideas?

Step one: Scan the news. Nothing is as funny as what people do, unless it's what they do and then try to cover up. The story of foot tapping as a secret code for anonymous sex in a public bathroom intrigued the public. The socially conservative senator trying to pass his foot tapping off as a "wide stance" was fodder for many late-night, talk-show monologues.

We gave away the world's first bobble-foot doll.

Step two: Scan your brain and link it back to some aspect of your business that fits and then look for an opposite. In baseball, bobble-heads have been done a million times. But no one had ever done a bobble-foot. It was an opposite that worked because it referred to a well-known scandal about foot tapping.

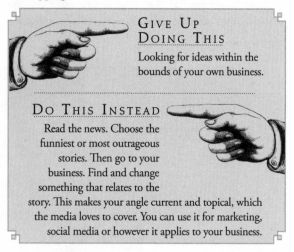

GIVE UP DOING THIS
Looking for ideas within the bounds of your own business.

DO THIS INSTEAD
Read the news. Choose the funniest or most outrageous stories. Then go to your business. Find and change something that relates to the story. This makes your angle current and topical, which the media loves to cover. You can use it for marketing, social media or however it applies to your business.

Great ideas and humor can come from the same principle: The opposite of what we expect. Outrageous also can mean funny.

CHAPTER 11

COMMITMENT

BE YOURSELF—THEN, WHEN THEY SIGN THE
PAPERS, YOU'LL GET A NICE LONG REST

WHEN A TELEMARKETER CALLS, I SAY, "PLEASE HOLD" AND HUM A KENNY G SONG

BY ALLEN FAHDEN

Then, I say, "Press One for English. Ess-pray Oo-tay for Ig-pay Atin-Lay." Then the telemarketers hang up on me.

Most people put energy into trying to be normal. Stop trying to be normal.

Most people put a lot of energy into trying to be normal. Normal means being the same as everyone else. But whether it's a job or a client you want, you need to stand out. Stop trying to be normal.

Look at your rivals. Find one thing they all do. Then do the opposite. Think of a way that being different helps your customer. Test it on a few prospects. If it works, do it with every lead. If it doesn't, don't give up. Try to be the opposite of your competitors on varying aspects of your offering until you find **your magic differentiator**.

GIVE UP DOING THIS

Benchmarking. Benchmarking? It means copying other companies. As someone once said, "That will put you on a treadmill to Bolivia."

DO THIS INSTEAD

The Internet makes every bit of knowledge available. So it's hard to do something no one's thought of. Instead, do something they wouldn't do.

You can tell if it's funny or just plain bad. How? Show your ideas to people in your target group. If they laugh, you have power.

CHAPTER 12

IMAGINATION
FABRICATE ALL THE ACCOMPLISHMENTS ON YOUR RESUME

WHAT POLISH
AMERICAN PRIDE
NIGHT TAUGHT
ME ABOUT
EXPECTATIONS

BY MIKE VEECK

A s senior vice president of marketing for the Tampa Bay Rays, I told a sports writer I was going to do a promotion at the stadium called Polish American Pride Night on a date when the team was on the road.

When you do things that are outrageous in a silly way, they shock the system.

Why schedule a game promotion when the team was on the road? The Polish American fans will show up to an empty ballpark and be mad as hell. Actually, no one got mad. It was so shocking for any team to do something like that that people just laughed—except for the Chicago-based National Polish Alliance. (Where's the largest concentration of Polish people outside Warsaw? Chicago, my hometown.) They didn't laugh. They wrote a lot of letters.

When you do things that are outrageous in a silly way, they shock the system. Dr. Sidney Weinstein, Editor in Chief of the *International Journal of Neuroscience*, put EEGs on subjects and then showed them out-of-the box messages.

He found that his subjects had to go into the right side of their brain to process them. And he found that once his subjects concentrated from their right brain, they liked the message better.

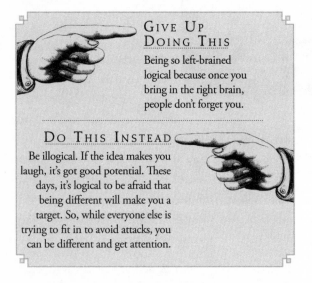

GIVE UP DOING THIS

Being so left-brained logical because once you bring in the right brain, people don't forget you.

DO THIS INSTEAD

Be illogical. If the idea makes you laugh, it's got good potential. These days, it's logical to be afraid that being different will make you a target. So, while everyone else is trying to fit in to avoid attacks, you can be different and get attention.

When you shock the system by forcing your viewers into their right brain, you get their attention and even get them talking about you.

CHAPTER 13

SYNERGY

YES, 1+1 IS MORE THAN 2, BUT ONLY IF
YOU KEEP THE BOOKS FOR ENRON

ARE YOU A
ROCKS FAN OR
A ROX FAN?

BY MIKE VEECK

We owned a new team in Brockton, Massachusetts. I wanted to name it after Rocky Marciano, the great heavyweight champ, who grew up there. But I was stuck between naming the team the Rocks, as in Rocky, or the Rox, as in the nearby Red Sox. Then I told Fahden, "Let's call it both names."

We laughed. Then we said, "Why not? How can we make it work?" Fahden quickly roughed out how both names could work on the uniforms. The shortstop would wear the word

Rocks on his uniform, and the second baseman would wear the word Rox.

What can you do with this? When people see something fun or weird at a stadium, they want to wear it on T-shirts. On the two opening nights, we broke all records for merchandise. We sold out of jerseys at $100 apiece.

Not bad for a team suffering from chronic ambivalence.

Everytime something makes you laugh, ask yourself, "What if I did that?"

GIVE UP DOING THIS

Dismissing things that make you laugh as frivolous and off target. A laugh is one step away from a big idea.

DO THIS INSTEAD

Every time something makes you laugh, ask yourself, "What if I did that? It's funny and stupid. How could I use this in my business? What if I made my customers laugh? Would they hate me, or embrace me?"

If it makes you laugh, it could be a revenue generator. Instead of dismissing what's funny, find a way to use it to grow your business.

CHAPTER 14

INTEGRITY
PUT PEOPLE ON HOLD FOR 20 MINUTES SO YOU CAN
SAVE $1.43 PER CALL CENTER AND THEN TELL THEM
THEIR CALL IS IMPORTANT TO YOU 200 TIMES

WHAT MY DAD'S OUTFIELD FENCE TAUGHT ME ABOUT INTEGRITY

by MIKE VEECK

"Today I'm going to teach you kids about integrity," my dad, Bill Veeck, said as he stood in outfield of the Cleveland Indians stadium. "Push on the fence." The Yankees were due in for a three-game series, the best home-run lineup in baseball. The Veeck kids pushed. The fence moved back on a rail, out of range of most fly balls. "Okay, lesson's over."

*If you want to do some good, ask yourself, "How can I do
something good by doing something evil?"
Then only do the ones that do good.*

You'd be shocked at how many opportunities you have if
you just change your thinking a little. Good pitchers will
make the hitters hit the ball a shorter distance. A great owner will make them hit the ball a longer distance. Which
costs less? A pitcher who can beat the Yankees, or a move-
able fence?

GIVE UP DOING THIS

Obeying without question the unwritten rules of your business.

DO THIS INSTEAD

Write down these rules. Come up with ideas based on "What if we did the opposite? How could we do it in a way that benefits our customer, and gives us a win?" Then do the best ones that aren't currently illegal.

If you want to do some good, ask yourself, "How can I do something good by doing something evil?" Then only do the ones that do good.

CHAPTER 15

AIM HIGH
IT'S MORE FUN THAT AIMING SOBER

It's Hard to Redeem a Coupon When It Weighs 1500 Pounds

by Allen Fahden

Why put a coupon in the newspaper when you can put it 30 feet in the air on a billboard? Mike Veeck and I did exactly that, 1500 miles apart, years before we knew each other.

I had been working with outdoor advertising on billboards for a few years and was itching to do something that you would never expect on a billboard. I had a client who was a plumbing wholesaler. Such a boring product made me want to find a really creative approach. By taking something obvious, such as a coupon that a customer could redeem and then doing something unexpected with it—printing the coupon on a 9 x 20-foot billboard about 20 feet off the ground—we got attention. By making the coupon difficult to redeem because it was 9 x 20 feet and 20 feet in the air, the advertiser received great attention. The stunt landed him and his ad on the front page of the newspaper. Someone had scraped the coupon off the billboard and reassembled it in the parking lot of the plumbing company

What can you do with your media that makes absolutely no sense?

to redeem the $100 credit. Silly minds think alike, because I found out years later that Mike had done the same thing in Florida, ten years after my plumbing wholesaler, when he worked for the advertising agency Wexler, McCarran and Roth. Mike was completely unaware of my idea.

The agency's client, Dale Allen Clothing, gave away a free suit with the coupon on the billboard. A customer disassembled the entire billboard and presented the coupon, still on the frame, at the clothing store. The guy got his free suit. Everybody was happy—except the head of the company that owned the billboard. He wanted to sue the customer. Mike explained to him what it would cost him to buy the equivalent of all the free publicity he had received. Then everybody was happy.

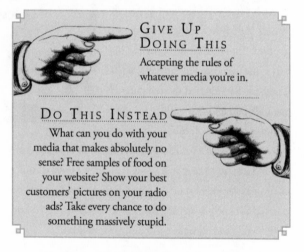

GIVE UP DOING THIS

Accepting the rules of whatever media you're in.

DO THIS INSTEAD

What can you do with your media that makes absolutely no sense? Free samples of food on your website? Show your best customers' pictures on your radio ads? Take every chance to do something massively stupid.

Google your smart idea. See that it's been done a million times. Now try a dumb idea. Almost no Google hits. How can you make that idea smart?

CHAPTER 16

BUSINESS MODEL INNOVATION
MAKE A BAD PRODUCT AND MAKE A FORTUNE FIXING IT

EVERYONE
HATES A MIME,
EXCEPT ME

BY MIKE VEECK

We called it Silent Night. We told the press we had an idea that would kill off the instant replay: mimes on the dugout roofs reenacting close plays. Our tag line for Silent Night: "Because a mime is a terrible thing to waste."

The crowd hated the mimes. They wanted to kill them. One guy hurled a hot dog at one of the mimes. At last, the crowd had finally found something entertaining about mimes. Soon concession food was sailing through the air as

the mimes covered their bodies with their hands in terror. We had the best food sales night in our history. We sent interns to the store three times for more hot dogs and buns.

I love mimes.

GIVE UP DOING THIS

Resisting the refiners who can tell you in advance what can go wrong. They're useful. They can fail your idea in the concept stage when it's cheap and easy to fix.

DO THIS INSTEAD

Next time a refiner tells you what can go wrong with your idea, ask a creator, "How can that be a good thing?" Or better yet, hire a mime to act out how it could be a good thing. I'll sell you the hot dogs.

Remember to ask, "What can go right?" You've heard of the law of unintended consequences? It's not just a good idea. It's the law.

CHAPTER 17

ABOVE AND BEYOND

THANK CONGRESS FOR GOING ABOVE ITS
CREDIT LIMIT AND BEYOND ITS MEANS

WHAT OUR BUTTE, MONTANA, TEAM TAUGHT ME ABOUT THE REAL COMPETITION

BY MIKE VEECK

"What would it take to get you out to a game?" we asked the 20-somethings in a local bar, who had never attended our minor-league team's games. They stared blankly at us.

We looked around the full bar and thought about our empty ballpark.

*Why fight our
potential market?*

Why fight our potential market? We turned the ballpark into a bar.

Every Friday night we pulled a semi trailer, full of beer, outside the left field wall and packaged the game ticket with dollar beers. Worst seats in the house, and nobody cared. We broke the all-time attendance record for the season.

GIVE UP
DOING THIS

Most marketers hurt themselves
by thinking their competition
only includes businesses in the
same category they are in.

DO THIS INSTEAD

What's your field? Now zoom out
one level from the customers' view.
Our view: Baseball—zoom out to
sports. Customers' view: Zoom out
to entertainment. Big difference.

*If you don't know what to do, ask your customers what
they want. The farther away what they want is from what
you presently do, the better the idea you can make it.*

CHAPTER 18

CUSTOMER DELIGHT

IF YOU WISH TO SPEAK HINDI, PRESS 2

PERFECTLY PC: THE INDIANS, GAY DIVORCE NIGHT AND SNEAKO DE MAYO

BY ALLEN FAHDEN

Some of my rejected baseball promotion ideas that still make me giggle:

THE INDIANS

No, no, not those Indians, the other Indians, the ones from *India*.

Have a frog file for all the ideas that suck today. They may help you leap tomorrow.

The idea was to combine the American outsourcing trend (crisis) with the unfortunately politically incorrect ball-team names peppered across professional, college and amateur sports teams in America. We would laugh with our fans at a profoundly stupid, silly idea: An outsourced baseball team. People get to the ballpark, and no one's on the field. The team calls the whole game in from Bangalore over the PA system in a melodic Indian accent:

"I just hit the ball."

"You did not. I struck you out."

GAY DIVORCE NIGHT

With a 50 percent divorce rate among the public at large, we figured that a few of the trendy new gay marriages were bound to end. That's the time to give them presents. Wedding showers make no sense. Two people, each owning a blender, get married. So you give them a third blender? Instead, have a divorce shower. That's when two people have only one blender and need another one. Invite gay people getting divorced to the ballpark and give a blender to anyone who can show proof that he or she has filed for divorce.

SNEAKO DE MAYO

On May 5 every year, if you can get into the ballpark without being caught, you get free education and medical care, and you pay no taxes. If you give birth that night in the ballpark, your kid gets a free season ticket for life. Out of fear of being considered racist, this offer would only be open to Minnesota-born Lutherans.

GIVE UP DOING THIS

Having people screen ideas for you. They throw out all the ideas that have something wrong with them, and you see only the derivative crap.

DO THIS INSTEAD

Every day, think about the worst ideas you can. Solicit them from your employees and think them up yourself. Give prizes for the dumbest and the funniest. Then ask, "What if we did something like this? How could we twist it to make it a win?"

To find a prince, you have to kiss a lot of frogs. Be sure to have a frog file for all the ideas that suck today. They may help you leap tomorrow.

CHAPTER 19

CONFIDENCE

YOU'LL FAIL, BUT YOUR DEODORANT WON'T

OPENING DAY
FIREWORKS—
IN A DOME?

BY MIKE VEECK

It was a beautiful display—until the sixth inning when the center fielder lost a routine pop fly in the cloud of smoke hanging over the outfield. Now I know why teams don't shoot off fireworks in a dome. Once that ball hit the turf, my debut as the senior vice president of marketing for the Tampa Bay Rays went up in smoke.

Even when you're doing the right thing, it can go wrong. Then it's all about how you handle it. In answer to the question, "Why would you do something like that?" I said it was a tribute to Jimi Hendrix. Then, I apologized. Maybe that wasn't enough.

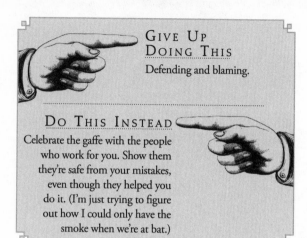

GIVE UP DOING THIS

Defending and blaming.

DO THIS INSTEAD

Celebrate the gaffe with the people
who work for you. Show them
they're safe from your mistakes,
even though they helped you
do it. (I'm just trying to figure
out how I could only have the
smoke when we're at bat.)

*One thing that can protect you from an idea that
bombs is your apology. Take responsibility and
say, "I'm sorry." Your critics will be stunned.*

CHAPTER 20

COMMUNITY
BORROW SOMEONE ELSE'S URINE FOR TODAY'S DRUG TEST

"WHILE YOU WAIT, WOULD YOU PREFER FORTUNE, FORBES OR MEDICAL ASPECTS OF HUMAN SEXUALITY?"

BY ALLEN FAHDEN

A s senior vice president of a large advertising agency, I noticed that others with corner offices had
Fortune, *Forbes* and *Business Week* on their coffee

194

If you want to get away with being crazy, look as sane as possible.

tables. I like to be different. So I got the most bizarre magazines I could find for my corner office. *American Funeral Director, Hog Farm Management* and *Diseases of the Colon and Rectum.*

Everything else was as corporate as I could make it. I wore a three piece, blue-pinstripe, vested suit and a very small patterned tie. If you want to get away with being crazy, look as sane as possible. Albert Mehrabian's studies say we register 55 percent of our information via our eyes. The more risky the idea I wanted to sell, the more I would dress up.

GIVE UP DOING THIS

Next time someone comes to you with an idea, don't fold your arms, no matter how risky the idea. When you say you like the idea, with your arms folded, people read your body language to mean that you hate the idea—and worse yet, that you're lying to them.

DO THIS INSTEAD

Open up your body posture. It will show you as someone who's open to creativity and innovation far better than anything you can say.

You can kill an idea with a look. Next time you feel like rolling your eyes, think of the damage you'll do. Be conscious of what you are telling people visually.

CHAPTER 21

DRIVE
BUT NOT DURING WORK WHEN YOU'RE DRUNK

WHAT THE MAGIC
BLACK BOX
TAUGHT ME ABOUT
HUMAN NATURE

BY MIKE VEECK

I had an idea so good that no one wanted it. Every kid wants to outdo his old man. My dad invented the exploding scoreboard. I decided to blow up the whole ballpark.

Allen and I made a plan for an exploding ballpark. When someone hit a homer, we would shoot a rocket in the path of the home-run ball all the way over the fence. Then we planned to play sounds of rumbling nuclear blasts that would shake the fans. When the runner trotted around the bases, blue smoke would come out of first base, red smoke out of second and green smoke out of third. While an inflatable marching band played behind the outfield stands, we would project images on the smoke and shoot sponsors' products out of confetti cannons. All the while, strobe lights and fireworks would make the ball field dance like a high-scoring video game. Too subtle? My inspiration was my son's fascination with the number-one competitor for his attention: video games.

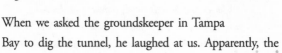

For a while we even thought of digging a tunnel from home plate to the dugout. As the runner neared the end of his home-run trot, smoke would pour out of home plate and he would disappear through a trap door and then mysteriously walk out of the dugout and wave to the fans.

When we asked the groundskeeper in Tampa Bay to dig the tunnel, he laughed at us. Apparently, the home plate at Tropicana Field was below the water table. Didn't see that one coming.

You can get some of your best ideas from imitating your competitor, especially if he's outside your category.

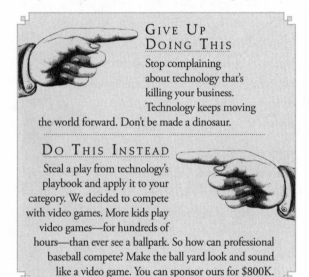

GIVE UP DOING THIS

Stop complaining about technology that's killing your business. Technology keeps moving the world forward. Don't be made a dinosaur.

DO THIS INSTEAD

Steal a play from technology's playbook and apply it to your category. We decided to compete with video games. More kids play video games—for hundreds of hours—than ever see a ballpark. So how can professional baseball compete? Make the ball yard look and sound like a video game. You can sponsor ours for $800K.

Who or what is your enemy outside your business category? Ask how you can do what your enemy does. The juice is in changing contexts.

CHAPTER 22

INSPIRATION
IT TOOK ALL I HAD JUST TO GET HERE TODAY

WHAT I LEARNED ABOUT CREATIVE ACCOUNTING FROM ARTHUR ANDERSEN APPRECIATION NIGHT

BY ALLEN FAHDEN

Right after the Enron scandal, I sold the AAA minor-league Portland team on Arthur Andersen Appreciation Night, honoring the Big Eight accounting firm that allegedly cooked Enron's books. This

*Treat every complaint as the
golden opportunity it is.*

was the deal at the ballpark: You pay $5 to get in, but we give you a receipt for $10 for tax purposes.

We threw in some other dubious Enron practices to continue the theme. "Bring your incriminating papers. Free shredders are located in every section of the stadium." We announced the attendance as 356,493 in a ballpark that only sat 19,000 and then rounded it down every inning. Then we announced recalculated numbers for the attendance for three days afterward.

Dangerous idea? More than we knew. We forgot to check with the refiners about what could go wrong. Turns out the title sponsor of the stadium was PG&E, an energy company owned by Enron. They let us know that they would have appreciated a warning before they saw our silly little promotion on CNN and ESPN.

Then 2000 people called or e-mailed to tell us how heartless we were for making fun of the people who had just lost their jobs. "Is it those people or the perpetrators we're roasting?" we asked. In every case, they agreed it was the latter. "And by the way," many of the callers added. "It was really funny."

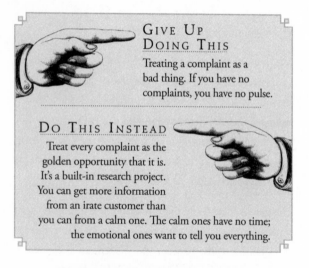

GIVE UP
DOING THIS

Treating a complaint as a bad thing. If you have no complaints, you have no pulse.

DO THIS INSTEAD

Treat every complaint as the golden opportunity that it is. It's a built-in research project. You can get more information from an irate customer than you can from a calm one. The calm ones have no time; the emotional ones want to tell you everything.

When you're idea looks safe, that's when it can be most dangerous. There's only one thing worse than being mistaken: being irrelevant.

CHAPTER 23

EXCELLENCE

A NEVER-ENDING QUEST FOR PERFECTION,
MOTIVATED BY THE KNOWLEDGE THAT EVERYONE
GETS A BIG TROPHY JUST FOR PARTICIPATING

What I Learned about Landing on Your Feet from the Detroit Tigers' 0–19 Start and the Naturally Appropriate Exorcism That Followed

BY MIKE VEECK

In the year 2000, the second year of the new Comerica Park, the Detroit Tigers had gotten off to such a bad start that the church across the street had a sign reading, "Pray for the Tigers."

I always have said, "Answer all your letters." So when a Native American tribal chief wrote me to say the new ballpark had been built on an ancient Indian burial ground, I believed him.

He offered to do an exorcism for us. When I told Tigers president Dave Dombrowski about the idea, he said, "Are you out of your mind? The media will kill us. Don't even think about it. *Don't do it!*"

But the chief was persistent. He called and assured us that we could get back on the winning track in a very private way. After we'd lost 18 of our first 19 games, I thought it was worth a shot.

So I arranged for the chief and two or three of his tribal assistants to get into the ballpark, while I ducked out to my home in Charleston for the weekend. Plausible deniability.

I don't know who left that stadium gate open.

Little did I know that right next door that day, at Ford Field, the Detroit Lions were introducing their new NFL uniforms during a press conference. Worse yet, all the reporters could look down from the less-than-captivating, uniform-launch, press conference right into our park to witness four Native Americans in full headdress, chanting and ritually exorcising the spirits from the pitcher's mound.

I swear I didn't plan for this publicity ambush. No...*really!*

Spying an elaborate, unpublicized tribal ceremony in a baseball park, the press swiftly abandoned the NFL fashion show. They had to uncover whatever ludicrous stunt Mike Veeck had cooked up now.

The news photographers snapped artistic shots of the tribe's religious machinations around the pitcher's mound with the contrasted backdrop of Tigers stadium to drive the absurdity home.

Meanwhile, Dave, who was supposed to be out of town, heard about my act of defiance.

So I told the chief I had made a big mistake and why. He laughed and told me about his nation's treaty with the United States. Turns out, he can legally kill any media coverage of any religious ceremony.

The story never ran. Even better: the Tigers actually won some games.

GIVE UP
DOING THIS
Being so afraid of
getting in trouble.

DO THIS INSTEAD
When you screw up, admit it early
and often. Then have some trust
that you might just be surprised.
What you don't know you don't
know may jump in to save the day.

Even if you fail your idea at first—in concept—you can still be blindsided by a bad outcome. But you can also be blindsided by a good one.

CHAPTER 24

START TODAY

THE JOURNEY OF A THOUSAND MILES BEGINS WITH
AIRPORT SECURITY LOOKING UP YOUR BUTT

What I Learned about Starting Today from Mr. Blue, the Talking Bird

by Mike Veeck

Here's the idea: One night we bring in a cockatiel we call Mr. Blue. We hang his cage up behind home plate and have him call balls and strikes over the PA system just to harass the umpire.

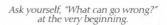

Ask yourself, "What can go wrong?"
at the very beginning.

Great idea, we thought. So we started on
the day we had the idea. We found a cockatiel trainer, booked him and that was it.

Or so we thought. Mr. Blue shows up with his trainer on
game night with an extensive vocabulary: The trainer had
taught him to say "Ball," "Strike," "What? Are you nuts?"
Brilliant.

Just one problem. Cockatiels are afraid of crowds.

Once the game started, Mr. Blue clammed up tighter than
a mobster pleading the Fifth Amendment. He wouldn't so
much as chirp.

"Mr. Trainer, could you maybe have told us this before we
invited ESPN to fly in to film the promotion?"

Fortunately, it turns out ESPN said the mute bird would be
funnier than the original gag.

Give up doing this: Thinking your safest ideas are actually your safest ideas. Usually, they're the ones that blow up, not the crazy ones.

Do this instead: Ask "What can go wrong?" at the very beginning. But don't let any of the naysayers kill the idea.

GIVE UP DOING THIS

Thinking your safest ideas are actually your safest ideas. Usually, they're the ones that blow up, not the crazy ones.

DO THIS INSTEAD

Do this instead: Ask "What can go wrong?" at the very beginning. But don't let any of the naysayers kill the idea.

Sales guru Larry Wilson once said, "Pain is the difference between what we expect and what we get." When a safe idea goes bad, it hurts more.

CHAPTER 25

COURAGE

ANNOUNCING AT THE HOLIDAY PARTY THAT YOU LOST
THE PENSION FUND IN THE DERIVATIVES MARKET

215

What the Worst
Team in Baseball
Taught Me
about Courage

by Mike Veeck

One day during a low attendance streak for my
dad's team, the St. Louis Browns, a woman
called the ballpark and said, "I'm bringing a
group of 12. What time does the game start?"

The Browns, now known as the Baltimore Orioles, were a
major-league team but had a small staff, warranted by their
small fan following.

"12 people?" cried the receptionist, who happened to be my mother. "What time do you want it to start?"

"Can we still get good seats?"

"How about second base?" Mom shot back. "We haven't used it all year."

My dad didn't just turn lemons into lemonade. He scoured the horizon for lemon trees. He would tell me: "The only place to go from the bottom is up."

Hide your good points in the right way,
and your audience will find them for you.

GIVE UP DOING THIS

The common "wisdumb" says selling means saying the best thing about yourself.

But people have always been skeptical about people who only broadcast positive sales pitches about themselves. They know that nothing can be all good. They wonder what you are hiding.

DO THIS INSTEAD

Be self-effacing. Say the worst thing about yourself, and see what happens. The left brain can't stand a contradiction, so you go to the right side to process it. What happens?

People wonder what good thing you're hiding.

Hide your good points in the right way, and your audience will find them for you. Then, they'll become your biggest fans. After all, no one likes a braggart.

CHAPTER 26

MAKE YOUR MARK
THEN HIDE THE SPRAY CAN UNDER YOUR DESK

"CALL ME— HERE'S MY CARD"

BY ALLEN FAHDEN

Ever get tired of trying to convince everyone of how smart you are? I did. Besides, I knew that sooner or later they would figure out that I'm more idiot than savant. So when I hand people my business card, they usually glance at it, and do a double take. Then they laugh.

It reads: Another Dumbass Author.

The more you push others to like you, buy from you, hire you, the more you put them off. You come off as needy. But if you call out the elephant in the room—the unspoken thoughts of those you have just met, "Who is this guy? Oh, another dumbass author"—they will know you aren't there to smother them with neediness. You are there to be genuine, to laugh, and to talk about what is real about yourself, them, life, and even business.

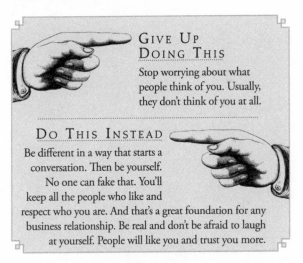

GIVE UP DOING THIS

Stop worrying about what people think of you. Usually, they don't think of you at all.

DO THIS INSTEAD

Be different in a way that starts a conversation. Then be yourself. No one can fake that. You'll keep all the people who like and respect who you are. And that's a great foundation for any business relationship. Be real and don't be afraid to laugh at yourself. People will like you and trust you more.

If you want the right customers, make the joke on you. Admit your weak spots and drive away those who will become your worst clients.

CHAPTER 27

CHALLENGE

PUTTING TOGETHER A COHERENT SENTENCE

WHAT BILL
VEECK'S WOODEN
LEG TAUGHT ME
ABOUT TRUST

BY MIKE VEECK

My dad used to love to sit on the porch and impress the neighborhood kids. One of his favorite party tricks was to hammer a nail into his leg just below the knee. The kids had no idea it was a wooden leg. As he pounded the last quarter inch of sharp steel through his pants, he'd smile at the kids and say, "Now go home, and ask your dad if he can do this."

If my dad could laugh about the leg he lost in a war, believe me, there is humor in anything.

People don't expect you to mess with them. Do something irreverent and funny, with a straight face, and watch people wake up and take notice.

Bill Veeck always said, "Buy the worst ball club you can find." Think about that. When the only way is up, you can either be a hero, or laugh about your failures. Either way wins you a lot of friends.

GIVE UP DOING THIS

Try to not take all this too seriously. One of the worst enemies of our creativity is the need to be literal.

DO THIS INSTEAD

See the humor in everything. If my Dad could laugh about the leg he lost in a war, believe me, there is humor in anything.

The mind can only hold one thought at a time. Make it one that supports you. Find the humor and your whole world transforms.

CHAPTER 28

TEAMWORK

TWO OR MORE DUMBASSES WORKING TOGETHER TO PRODUCE A
RESULT NOT OBTAINABLE BY ANY ONE DUMBASS INDEPENDENTLY

227

WEAK ANKLES CAN MAKE
A STRONG MESSAGE

BY ALLEN FAHDEN

When the Dallas Stars of the NHL were previously the Minnesota North Stars, their fans grumbled with disappointment after a bad season. So for their TV ad, I hired six guys who had never skated, dressed them in North Star uniforms and filmed them stepping onto the ice.

As their weak ankles collapsed them into a pile, the announcer said, "After last season, you're probably expecting this. Instead, we're working hard enough to give you this" (cut to dramatic slow motion shot of the real team hustling onto the ice).

*Take the criticism you're most afraid
of and accept it rather than resist.*

GIVE UP DOING THIS

If people are criticizing you, stop resisting. Go with it. It's an old martial arts trick. Use the force of the attackers against them to propel them in the direction they're already going.

DO THIS INSTEAD

Take the criticism you're most afraid of and accept it rather than resist. There's always an angle to it that won't necessarily hurt you. Then add a positive outcome for yourself. You'll create the perception that you've corrected your fault, and you're better off than ever.

You can actually gain more ground by making a mistake and then making up for it in a happy way. Try new things. You can only gain.

CHAPTER 29

SERVICE
TELL YOUR CUSTOMERS THEY'RE LYING AND
THEN ASK THEM TO FILL OUT A SURVEY

WHAT I LEARNED ABOUT TRUTH FROM CHIA PET NIGHT

by MIKE VEECK

Why is it that the Chia Pet industry has sold millions, but no one has ever admitted to buying one? So when we had Chia Pet Night and torched a six-foot-tall Chia Pet, a cute little animal made out of geraniums, we were pretty sure no one would show up.

We were wrong. Four thousand people flocked to the game, most likely just to lay their eyes on some fool who had bought a Chia Pet. We already knew that customers don't always do what they say they're going to do. But we didn't know until that night that they also do things they'll refuse to admit.

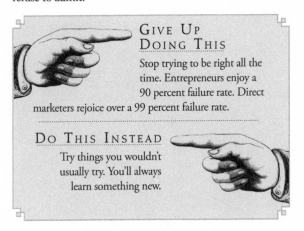

GIVE UP DOING THIS

Stop trying to be right all the time. Entrepreneurs enjoy a 90 percent failure rate. Direct marketers rejoice over a 99 percent failure rate.

DO THIS INSTEAD

Try things you wouldn't usually try. You'll always learn something new.

People learn more from failures. Think about this. Maslow says we pay more attention to threats than opportunities. Fail more; learn more.

Try things you wouldn't usually try. You'll always learn something new.

CHAPTER 30

BELIEVE AND SUCCEED

BELIEVE YOU'RE SMARTER THAN EVERYONE
AND SUCCEED AT BEING A SCUMBAG

What Lawyer Appreciation Night Taught Me about the Humor-Impaired

BY MIKE VEECK

When I announced to my staff at the Tampa Bay Rays that we were going to do Lawyer Appreciation Night, it was met with deathly silence. Here's the deal. If you were a lawyer, and came to the Tampa Bay Rays game that night, you had to pay double to get in. Then we billed you in 15-minute increments, and marked up the concessions just for you.

Pick the right target and you can get people on your side no matter what.

We had a hanging judge stationed down the third base line.

The St. Petersburg Bar loved the idea.

So did the Tampa Bar.

The Clearwater Bar? They sent me a scathing letter saying lawyers didn't need more lawyer jokes. I guessed they definitely wouldn't sponsor it. Too bad.

People don't understand that if they can laugh at themselves, and admit their little flaws, it makes others like them more. Laughing at yourself can stop your detractors because they have nothing to attack when you are already part of the joke about yourself.

I got a call from a bunch of Philadelphia lawyers, who said, "Get the local lawyers to play us in an exhibition game, and we'll contribute $10,000 to the ACLU," for whom we were doing the fundraiser.

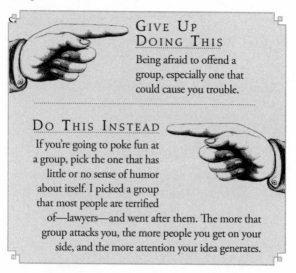

GIVE UP DOING THIS

Being afraid to offend a group, especially one that could cause you trouble.

DO THIS INSTEAD

If you're going to poke fun at a group, pick the one that has little or no sense of humor about itself. I picked a group that most people are terrified of—lawyers—and went after them. The more that group attacks you, the more people you get on your side, and the more attention your idea generates.

Pick the right target and you can get people on your side no matter what. But don't be mean. Be silly.

CHAPTER 31

VISION

CLOSE ANOTHER PLANT—ENABLE THE LAUNCH
OF 28,000 MORE INTERNET MARKETERS

What My Blind Play-By-Play Announcer Taught Me about Vision

by Mike Veeck

If I could have, I'd have hired blind umpires. So when Don Wardlow, who had had no sight since birth, wanted a job as my radio announcer, I hired him on the spot. A few days later, I asked him how he was going to do it.

Seek out the people who are just a little different for one reason or another.

Turns out he had a sighted, play-by-play partner. And once he heard what was happening on the field, he knew so much about baseball that he nailed the rest of it as the color commentator who added knowledge and insight to the discussion. It taught me a lot about how well people can do, no matter what their limitations seem to be.

Little did I know that, five years later, my daughter Rebecca would start to lose her sight from retinitis pigmentosa. My experience with the blind announcer shot me into action. She and I took the next six months off, seeing everything in the world that we could see before her sight went away. Every image from that trip is still etched in her brain.

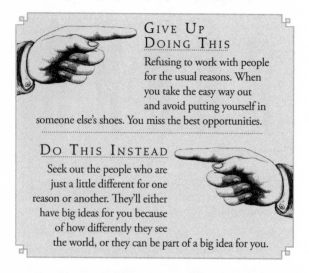

GIVE UP DOING THIS

Refusing to work with people for the usual reasons. When you take the easy way out and avoid putting yourself in someone else's shoes. You miss the best opportunities.

DO THIS INSTEAD

Seek out the people who are just a little different for one reason or another. They'll either have big ideas for you because of how differently they see the world, or they can be part of a big idea for you.

The best teams are the most diverse. Win with people who are different from you: creators, advancers, refiners and executors.

CHAPTER 32

DETERMINATION

TAKE A HIGH-PERFORMING OPERATION
AND RUN IT INTO THE GROUND

ENGLISH, FOR ME, IS A SECOND LANGUAGE—I DON'T HAVE A FIRST

BY ALLEN FAHDEN

Just because you learned something early in life doesn't mean you should cling to it blindly forever. I scored As in French in high school. So 20 years later, I went to France and spoke no English. I was determined that my stellar high-school French would get me by. Yet, no one seemed to understand a word I said.

After five days of "Parrrrdonne?" I gave up. In a Paris shop I finally had enough. "Do you speak English?" I asked the shopkeeper who had stared at me blankly as I gave her my best French vocabulary.

"Ah, yes," the chic sales lady assured me. "But I um so surprased that yuu duu. I thought you were Czech."

Turns out all the French I learned from my Czech, refugee, high-school French teacher was laced with the same heavy Slavic accent he had when he spoke English. The English version of my pidgin French would have sounded like: "Iss pleez fur tu heff cookie?"

If someone had just told me that my teacher's heavy Slavic accent in English might also show up in French, I would have not spent 20 years in a delusion about my language skills.

The safer your action looks, the more you should ask your refiners and executors what can go wrong.

GIVE UP DOING THIS

If it's a normal idea that looks safe enough, stop assuming it's going to go well.

DO THIS INSTEAD

The safer your action looks, the more you should ask your refiners and executors what can go wrong.

One hundred percent of the work today (finish what you start) is for only 1 percent of the people, who are the only ones who naturally do all the phases of the work. Instead, hand off from one core work nature to the next.

CHAPTER 33

NEVER QUIT

WAIT TO BE FIRED—YOU GET MORE

A CLIENT ONCE TOLD ME: "FAHDEN, IF YOU WERE MY LAWYER, I'D BE IN THE ELECTRIC CHAIR"

BY ALLEN FAHDEN

My client said this after I had spent his whole ad budget on printing the billboards I had created. He had no money left to rent billboard space.

A huge mistake. But there is a deeper lesson. He and I looked the same, but we didn't think the same. I'm a creator. I shake things up with my ideas. To me, the idea was everything. He was a refiner. He wanted to protect the system from bad ideas. He won't do something until it's proven that it won't go wrong. He was most concerned about avoiding any bad consequences.

Knowing your own core nature and that of those around you reveals who should be in which role. We all see things in different ways. It's our core nature. To make this easy to get, we give you four of them: advancer, creator, refiner, executor. I'm a creator. I should never be in charge of the money.

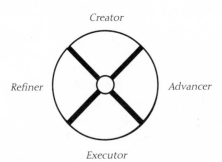

Knowing your own core nature and that of those around you reveals who should be in which role.

GIVE UP DOING THIS

Involving everyone in all phases of the work.

DO THIS INSTEAD

Go to the natural early adopters first. Once you understand the way each person does her work, you can get a lot more projects to the finish line—good, fast and cheap. Advancers are natural starters and thinkers. Creators are natural starters and doers. Refiners are natural finishers and thinkers. Executors are natural finishers and doers. If you reorder who does what, based on their core natures, you can double or even triple your output.

Realize that people are different. Their strengths make up four different core natures. Put them in the right place at the right time doing the right thing, and you've reinvented work for the twenty-first century.

CHAPTER 34

CHANGE
IT'S WHAT'S LEFT AFTER TAXES

Do Not Resist Changing Your Underwear before Work—You Never Know When Someone Might Run over You

BY MIKE VEECK

L iving in Charleston and considering myself a literate man, I was delighted when *Midnight in the Garden of Good and Evil*, set in Savannah, Georgia, rode the best-seller list for more than 100 weeks.

I thought it would be fun the next time we played the dreaded Savannah Sand Gnats to capture that spirit on Voodoo Night. We gave away 500 little voodoo dolls, and 500 pins to stick in them.

We set it for Friday the Thirteenth. Ah. Savannah was coming to town: the Lady Chablis tribute with drag queens dragging the infield, the mystical voodoo promotion. What could possibly go wrong?

It turned out that year, this particular Friday the Thirteenth fell on Good Friday.

My wife, Libby, and co-owner Bill Murray both agreed: "They'll murder you. It's the stupidest idea you ever had."

I said, "I will not be faced down. I'm going to do this."

253

Like many creators, I had fallen in love with the idea. And like many creators, I did it despite the problems.

For the next two days, the phone lines melted. Finally, I called a press conference for the first time in my life and said, "I'm sorry. I'm stupid and I'll make sure it never happens again."

People adopt ideas in companies much like they adopt products in their own lives. This means, if you take your hot new program to a late adopter, she's going to push back, and tell you what's going to go wrong. Or worse, she'll just do something that doesn't at all resemble your original idea.

But in this case, both Libby and Bill are early adopters. The lesson: when an early adopter doesn't like an idea, get really specific about why, and brainstorm ideas for removing the problem without killing the idea.

Was the Savannah team coming to town later in the season? If not, could voodoo night be done the next year? Maybe waiting is a problem, because the book may have passed its prime.

GIVE UP
DOING THIS

By going to late adopters first,
you're losing new ideas to their
skepticism. It's their nature to tell
you what's wrong, and they're
not going to give you a better idea to replace it, just one
that's more tried and true and therefore more ordinary.

DO THIS INSTEAD

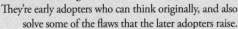

Go to your early adopters first.
Advancers can tell you which idea
has the best chance of success and
how to get it implemented. If you
need more ideas, go to creators.
They're early adopters who can think originally, and also
solve some of the flaws that the later adopters raise.

*Treat your own company people like a market. They
buy ideas just the way they buy products. Start
with the early adopters and they'll do the rest.*

CHAPTER 35

GOALS

WORK HARD AND YOU COULD BE THE BEST
GREETER IN WALMART HISTORY

BAT NIGHT WITH
TONYA HARDING

BY MIKE VEECK

Tonya Harding's husband allegedly had her Olympic rival hit in the knees with a baseball bat. So, Tonya Harding, combined with baseball's traditional promotion, Bat Night, was a no-brainer. We didn't mention to Ms. Harding that she was coming in for Bat Night. She was a great sport and signed every minibat in sight, even though her contract stated, "no mention of black batons." I was giggling.

Most people shun those who get bad press. I embrace them. If you make people laugh at the absurdity of life, and you laugh at yourself in the process, your brand will soar.

Think about all the ideas your competitors fear. Then try one. Test it first. If customers laugh, you're onto something. If they say you're crazy, ask them why. If they can't give you a specific answer, you have a winner. Rethink what can go wrong. Ask refiners. Those are the people whose core work nature is to see around corners to tell you what will go wrong. If nothing can go wrong, it's a boring idea. Retest and then move forward despite your fear.

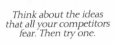

Think about the ideas that all your competitors fear. Then try one.

GIVE UP DOING THIS

Killing ideas that scare you,
or scare people around you.

DO THIS INSTEAD

1. **Test for clarity.** Does she
get it? If she doesn't, ask her
what it means to her. Then, tell
her what you want it to mean,
and ask what you can say for
her to get that meaning.

2. **Test for taste.** This is tougher. Many people say
something is offensive because they think it will offend
someone else. This kills most ideas. It shouldn't. Any
idea that has impact is going to offend someone.
The only question is how many and whom?

*When refiners and executors tell you they don't like
your idea, ask them to be specific. Then take that specific problem to a creator and ask him to solve it.*

CHAPTER 36

FOCUS
GO FOC YOURSELF

You'd Be Surprised
by the Kind of
Intelligence People
Show When You
Just Let Them

Sixty years ago my dad, Bill Veeck, may have accidentally invented crowd sourcing.

When he owned the St. Louis Browns in 1951, he decided to let the fans manage a game.

He publicly scolded his manager, Zachary Taylor, for being so bad that the crowd could do a better job.

That Sunday, Taylor sat in front of the dugout in a rocking chair, having no contact with the players. Meanwhile, the team issued large signs to the first thousand customers who arrived. On one side, each sign displayed, in giant letters, "Yes." On the other side, "No."

In the third inning, the Browns got a rare runner on first base. My dad held up his own sign to the crowd: "Steal?" Then, he counted the yes and no answers. "Yes" won, so he gave the runner the steal sign.

In that game, he also held up the "Bunt?" card as well as several others, each time implementing the crowd's decision.

263

The Browns won.

Ideas like this don't come from focus. They don't come from "sticking to the knitting." They come from a delicious combination of challenging the present and dreaming of the future. They come from being a creator. Creators invented ADD and ADHD. Not the diagnosis, but the actual symptoms.

The creator's credo: We don't focus, and you can't make us. Go ahead and try. Sorry, can't look at you for very long. I'm attracted to shiny objects.

That's because it's my nature to scan for places to implement my ideas and for problems my ideas can solve. If you use me right, I can fuel the company with ideas and breakthrough thinking. If you force me to be who I'm not, you will get work that is bad, slow and expensive.

If you come to me for ideas, solutions and concepts for process innovation and then hand off my ideas to advancers to implement, you will get work that is better, faster and cheaper than you ever imagined.

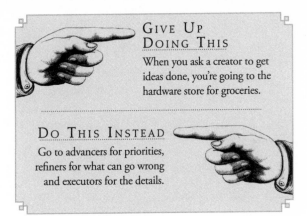

GIVE UP
DOING THIS

When you ask a creator to get ideas done, you're going to the hardware store for groceries.

DO THIS INSTEAD

Go to advancers for priorities, refiners for what can go wrong and executors for the details.

Unlike the early adopters (creators and advancers), the later adopters (refiners and executors) will identify the barriers early in the process, when they're faster, easier and cheaper to fix.

CHAPTER 37

WALK THE TALK

DON'T JUST SAY SOMETHING STUPID; BET
THE WHOLE COMPANY ON IT

"RAIL TRAVEL AT HIGH SPEED IS NOT POSSIBLE BECAUSE PASSENGERS, UNABLE TO BREATHE, WOULD DIE OF ASPHYXIA"

(PROFESSOR DIONYSUS LARDNER)

BY ALLEN FAHDEN

If you bet the company on making only incremental changes, the innovators in other companies will take all your customers away.

When I started out creating advertising, one rule you could never break was that billboards had to be short—never more than seven words.

One day, my client, Cedric's Clothing, bought a billboard on France Avenue, in Edina, Minnesota, one of the most crowded streets in the whole Minneapolis area.

So I approached him with an idea that was really stupid. It broke the most basic rules of outdoor advertising: a 40-word billboard. It read something like this:

> If you're moving slowly enough to read this,
> tell the driver you'll meet him at Seventieth Street,
> jump out of the car, walk two blocks north, shop at Cedrics
> and get back in the car at the next stop light.

Cedric looked at the layout, laughed and said, "Let's run it." My favorite client.

Every new idea draws naysayers from the ranks of its later adopters. Leaders will often listen and abandon ideas. Why? Harvard Business School Professor Teresa Amabile found in a study of book reviews that people writing negative reviews were perceived as smarter than people writing positive reviews.

Leaders will often listen to naysayers and abandon ideas.

GIVE UP
DOING THIS

Don't put the fox in
charge of the hen house,
or you're in for trouble.

DO THIS INSTEAD

Make sure your company is
organized to let the natural
progression from early adopters
to late adopters work inside your
business as well as it naturally
does outside in the market. This
means taking all the parts of
your business you want to stay the same or become more
efficient, and putting the refiners and executors in charge.
Take the parts where you need to innovate and attract new
customers, and put the advancers and creators at the helm.

*Get the creators and advancers driving innovation and
change, and gain new revenue. Keep the refiners and executors running the system for efficiency and more profit.*

CHAPTER 38

DEPRESSION

DON'T CALL IN SICK; CALL IN WITH A VAGUE SENSE OF DOOM

It's rarely about
what we think
it's about

by Allen Fahden

When Bud Grant coached the Minnesota Vikings, he had a stereotype that people talked about but no one ever harnessed: He never laughed in public.

People would call him things like "Stone Face." I loved that and wanted to use it as a powerful bit of communication.

I had a simple idea. Take any product or service that was more fun than its competition, show Bud Grant using it, and then make him laugh as hysterically as humanly possible.

No one had ever seen him do this before, so I had to sell this idea. Unfortunately, it was removed enough from what people expected to make it an easy target for idea killers.

And it was.

It took me five no's from different clients to sell that idea. Finally, Farrell's Ice Cream went with it, because fun was already their market position.

The Bud Grant Farrell's spot was a huge hit. People talked about it for years.

Bulletproof your idea as fast as you can. Raise objections. Fix them.

Use your refiners to tell you what can go wrong, and have your executors tell you how it can disrupt the system.

Then use your advancers and creators to fix the problems. This will save you lots of headaches down the road when you install your idea in the company.

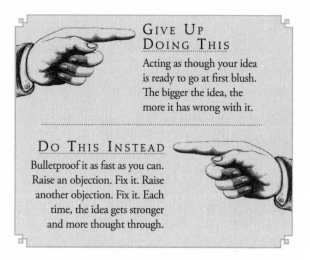

GIVE UP DOING THIS

Acting as though your idea is ready to go at first blush. The bigger the idea, the more it has wrong with it.

DO THIS INSTEAD

Bulletproof it as fast as you can. Raise an objection. Fix it. Raise another objection. Fix it. Each time, the idea gets stronger and more thought through.

You can innovate much faster once you get a tennis match going between the early adopters (advancers and creators) and later adopters (refiners and executors.)

CHAPTER 39

DIVERSITY

BLACK, WHITE, GAY, STRAIGHT—YOU'RE STILL AN ASSHOLE

277

YOU'RE ALWAYS GOING TO OFFEND SOMEBODY, SO AT LEAST MAKE IT A GROUP OF PEOPLE WHO ARE AFRAID TO IDENTIFY THEMSELVES

BY ALLEN FAHDEN

When we sold these demotivational posters to a giant greeting card company, the refiners and executors said, "You can't use the diversity poster. You'll offend too many people." That's when my partner, Mark, an advancer, said, "What do you care whom you offend? You don't have any business anyway."

Who's going to call and say, "Hey, I'm an asshole and I resent that"?

Besides, when you criticize assholes, who's going to call and say, "Hey, I'm an asshole and I resent that"?

So we went ahead, and guess what? Diversity became our biggest seller.

If you're starting a business, launching a new product or even trying to get a new market for an old one, remember one thing about early adopters: You can do things with them that break all the rules. Why? They hate rules. They're attracted to the new and different. And in this age of political correctness, nothing is newer and more different than irreverence.

GIVE UP DOING THIS

Taking your ideas to just anyone. You have an 85 percent chance of being shot down. Why? Creators, who make up 35 percent of the population, want you to do their idea instead. Refiners (25 percent) see too many things that can go wrong. Executors (25 percent) see only the damage your idea will do to "the routine."

DO THIS INSTEAD

Next time you have some ideas, go to only the advancers (15 percent). Ask two things:

- Which idea's the best and why? Save the rest of the ideas for other times.

- What are the next steps? Then follow those steps, or ask the advancers if they will.

Eighty-five percent of your people want to kill your idea. The better you know their core work nature, the better you'll know what to do with their comments.

CHAPTER 40

DREAM
WHEN YOU WAKE UP, YOUR 401K WILL BE GONE

WHAT "NOBODY NIGHT" TAUGHT ME ABOUT THE VALUE OF NOTHING

BY MIKE VEECK

We wanted to set a world record for single game attendance. My dad held the record in Cleveland for 80,241. Beating that was a tall order for a minor-league team. So we considered doing the opposite. We checked the record for the least fans. The Portland Beavers held it for a game when one person showed up. "Hey, we can beat that!" I decided. I'm an optimist.

So we sponsored Nobody Night. We didn't let any attendees inside the stadium until it was officially a "complete game." Attendance: 0. We served beer and hot dogs in the little park just beyond the outfield wall. The fans could look into the game with ladders, and get in after 5 ½ innings.

We weren't sure what to do in the ballpark during the game. Should the vendors even show up? Yes, we decided. The principle: Do something very different and then have everyone act as normally as they can. We had the vendors hawking to empty seats, and complaining about a slow night.

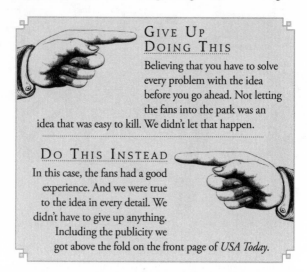

GIVE UP
DOING THIS

Believing that you have to solve
every problem with the idea
before you go ahead. Not letting
the fans into the park was an
idea that was easy to kill. We didn't let that happen.

DO THIS INSTEAD

In this case, the fans had a good
experience. And we were true
to the idea in every detail. We
didn't have to give up anything.
Including the publicity we
got above the fold on the front page of *USA Today*.

*When you have a novel idea, get the refiners and executors
to flesh it out. They will make sure the customer enjoys it.*

CHAPTER 41

COLLABORATE
TAKE A PERFECTLY SIMPLE IDEA AND ARGUE
IT UNTIL IT MAKES NO SENSE AT ALL

EVER BEEN IN A MEETING
WHEN IT'S ONE O'CLOCK, TWO
O'CLOCK, THREE O'CLOCK,
THREE O'CLOCK, THREE
O'CLOCK, THREE O'CLOCK...

BY MIKE VEECK

Sometimes, there's only one thing more dangerous than doing stupid ideas: doing smart ideas.

When we owned the Butte Copper Kings, we set up our promotional calendar on one of the few sure things in baseball: a July 1 fireworks display. We decided to give this Montana town of 40,000 the biggest show it had ever seen and at the same time set a new single game attendance record.

Find some later adopters you know and ask them what could go wrong with that. They'll probably say, "Nothing."

But just as a dangerous idea doesn't always go wrong, a safe idea doesn't always go right.

On July 1, Butte made national news. And it wasn't our fireworks display.

It was snow.

This was not possible. Worse, it was heavy, wet snow. And you can't physically shoot fireworks in a blizzard.

Twelve people showed up. But they expected fireworks. So with a total gate of $182, we delivered on the fireworks that cost $4500.

Could it get worse? Of course.

You shoot the fireworks from behind the outfield fence. Just before the show started, the snow fell even harder. The rockets never got higher than the eight-foot fence.

Who saw the fireworks? Only the guy who shot them off. He said it was very exciting. Of course, they were exploding two feet above his head.

So even refiners can't always see what's coming, especially if it's a freak of nature.

But make friends with refiners anyway. They don't have to kill your idea. In fact, they can show you what's going to go wrong so you can fix it in concept where it's easy, fast and cheap to fix. But if you find they take the wind out of your sails when you are in your first moments of enthusiasm, you can wait to ask for their concerns when the idea isn't so new and delicate. I like to tell them, "It's not time to refine the idea yet."

GIVE UP DOING THIS

Resisting the people who resist your ideas (refiners and executors).

DO THIS INSTEAD

Once you get an advancer to tell you which idea should be the biggest priority, do the opposite of what you'd usually do and ask the refiners to have at it. Don't argue, just write down their objections. Even though they might make you feel stupid, get their input anyway. By following their own ultracautious natures, the refiners are helping you to have an even better idea, as long as you solve its problems.

Refiners and executors will make your idea better. Just ask them for specific problems and then have your creators solve them with ideas.

CHAPTER 42

BRILLIANCE

GIVE THE STIMULUS MONEY TO BANKERS,
WHO WON'T LEND IT OUT

WHAT YOGI BERRA
TAUGHT ME ABOUT
BRILLIANCE

BY MIKE VEECK

When baseball legend Yogi Berra was in the eighth grade, he was not known for his academic prowess, and he definitely didn't test well. After Berra had scored particularly badly on one exam, his teacher gravely summoned Yogi to his desk.

"Lawrence, from the results of this test it doesn't seem that you know *anything*," he sternly admonished the future Hall of Famer.

"Know anything," replied Yogi. "I don't even suspect anything."

Yet, Lawrence "Yogi" Berra went on to become a legend in two of the most intellectually demanding positions in major-league baseball. As a 15-time, all-star, New York Yankee catch-

It ain't over until you've taken all the stupid ideas seriously.

er and three-time American League Most Valuable Player, he called the pitches to opposing hitters on the way to 10 world championships. Then, as a manager, the brains of the whole operation, he won championships in both leagues.

How could one of the most brilliant minds in baseball have struggled so much with basic concepts in school?

If success doesn't come from "knowing anything," there must be something else that allows a person to excel. When Berra was in the wrong place (school), he floundered. When he was in the right place, using his strengths (baseball), he flourished.

GIVE UP
DOING THIS

Trying to look smart all the time. You give up the other half of the ideas (the dumb half) where you stand the best chance of standing out.

DO THIS INSTEAD

Instead of trying to come up with a smart idea and then figuring out what can go wrong, come up with a stupid idea and then figure out what can go right.

It ain't over until you've taken the stupid ideas seriously. Illegal in 18 states? Then it's legal in 32 states. Launch in 32; lobby in 18.

CHAPTER 43

RISK

PUT THIS ON THE WALL—PRAY THAT NOBODY READS
IT AND FINDS OUT WHAT A PUTZ YOU ARE

ATTENTION,
BURGLARS

BY ALLEN FAHDEN

Some people think it's a risk to do things too publicly. My ad agency had been burglarized seven times. While we weren't located in a bad neighborhood, we were bad neighborhood adjacent. And we had no alarm system. So we decided to move to a building with a state-of-the-art security system. When we moved, we ran an ad in the daily paper: Attention, Burglars. Fahden As In Cat has moved to 430 Oak Grove.

Now, refiners would tell you that we were literally inviting people to burgle us. But they didn't. They knew where we were, but they couldn't break in. We were never broken into

Either give too much info or not enough. Both ways you can avoid risk and be different.

ATTENTION BURGLARS

at the new place. Burglars don't like to commute. But we did get a lot of attention, creative credit and new clients from our very visible laugh at our bad luck with burglars.

Later, my freelance creative partner at the time, Thom Sandberg, managed risk by using the same principle far more brilliantly. He put posters all over the city with his picture, but not his name. The only words were: "If you know me, you're invited to a party at my house, 7 p.m., June 23." Either give too much info or not enough. Both ways you can avoid risk and be different as well.

GIVE UP DOING THIS

Stop killing ideas that appear to have something wrong with them.

DO THIS INSTEAD

Look deeper into the idea and the circumstances. Sometimes there can be a mitigating factor that gives you a free pass, much like the football quarterback who sees a penalty flag and goes for a long pass knowing he has a free play. Why would you invite burglars in? A security system. Why would you invite strangers to your party? They don't know where you live.

Don't ever let an objection to an idea defeat you. There is always a way to make it work. Ask creators until you find out how.

CHAPTER 44

DO IT NOW

LATER YOU'LL BE TOO DRUNK

BASEBALL?
I HAVE TO ADMIT I'M A
MINNESOTA TWITS FAN

BY ALLEN FAHDEN

I n the 1980s a rather large number of Minnesota Vikings were getting caught for driving while intoxicated (DWI). So I took the Vikings logotype, changed just one thing, and put it on a sweatshirt: Minnesota DWIkings. I can't help myself. I'm an extreme creator. And to a creator, everything is an opportunity for an idea.

According to Marcus Buckingham, only 17 percent of people work their strengths at least once a week. Once a week. Yet, one study showed that people working their strengths beat the work goal by 15 percent, while people working their weaknesses fell short of the same goal by 30 percent.

GIVE UP
DOING THIS

Accepting work you don't do well just to be a team player. You hurt the team by doing this. You slow them down, get them off track and cause upsets.

DO THIS INSTEAD

If you're a creator, think up ideas and solve problems. If you're an advancer, set priorities (choose the best ideas) and make plans. If you're a refiner, warn people about what can go wrong. If you're an executor, dot the i's, cross the t's and keep the system well oiled—but not yourself because later, you'll be too drunk.

A creator will kill your idea for one reason: it's not hers. Instead, go to the creator to solve the barriers the late adopters raised.

CHAPTER 45

TEMPWORK
HIRE A TEMP AND MAKE HIM DO ALL THE WORK

WHAT A SMALL
CHAIN OF STEREO
STORES TAUGHT ME
ABOUT SCRAPPING
FOR SUCCESS

BY ALLEN FAHDEN

The guy who owned the stores called Sound of Music, told me his philosophy. "Always get up one more time than you've been knocked down." He had asked me to do a radio campaign to sell car stereos.

"How can we sell car stereos on the radio?" I whined. "We can't demonstrate them on someone's crappy car system."

He said, "That's what I'm paying you to figure out. And I need it this week."

After I got back up, I started thinking. If we can't sell the solution, let's sell the problem. In Minnesota, when the snow melts after months of slow, slippery driving, they tear up the roads to fix the potholes. This means you're stuck in your car for hours. You might as well have a good sound system. That made me come up with the line: "Minnesota's two seasons, winter and road construction." Not only did it sell car stereos, but also the line became Minnesota's unofficial slogan to discourage tourism. Then it spread to other northern states as well. At 1,040,000 hits on Google, it's not quite viral. But it did go bacterial.

Oh, and the guy who owned the stores? He kept getting up after he got knocked down. My little ad agency did his ads for years and even introduced him to TV advertising. In the early eighties Dick Schulze changed the name of his stores to Best Buy.

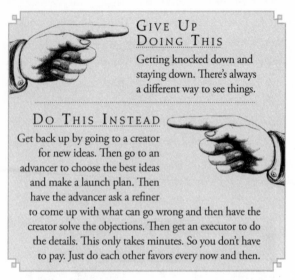

GIVE UP DOING THIS

Getting knocked down and staying down. There's always a different way to see things.

DO THIS INSTEAD

Get back up by going to a creator for new ideas. Then go to an advancer to choose the best ideas and make a launch plan. Then have the advancer ask a refiner to come up with what can go wrong and then have the creator solve the objections. Then get an executor to do the details. This only takes minutes. So you don't have to pay. Just do each other favors every now and then.

You don't have to have to hire a team. Just take your idea to the right strength at the right time. Trade favors and solve it in minutes.

CHAPTER 46

COOPERATION

SHARE ALL YOUR CRAP WORK WITH THE
PEOPLE WHO ANNOY YOU THE MOST

ONE PERSON'S CRAP IS ANOTHER PERSON'S CREPE

BY ALLEN FAHDEN

People are different. And often those different from us annoy us, confuse us and sometimes just plain piss us off. But on the bright side, the work that's boring and stressful to you might be kind of fun for someone else.

Unfortunately, differences in work priorities can be devastating if you put the wrong person in charge of major decisions. That person needs to have the same values and goals as the whole company.

Be careful about who works together and who doesn't.

We were testing some ideas for T-shirts for one of Mike's baseball teams, and had one design sell out of the team shop very fast. After hearing the good news from the executor who ran the test and was responsible for stocking the merchandise at the ballpark, I asked her, "How many of that design are you going to reorder?"

"Oh, I'm not going to order any more of those," she told me in a serious tone of voice.

"Um… Why not?" I asked, perplexed.

"Oh, they sold too well," she explained. "If I reordered that design, I'd just have to keep re-ordering it all the time."

"Um…" My mind boggled.

GIVE UP DOING THIS

Stop doing the phases of a
project that you hate and
naturally suck at doing.
But be careful. If you work
directly with someone whose strength is the opposite
of yours, you may get some surprising results.

DO THIS INSTEAD

If you're a creator, get an
advancer to do your priorities
and plan. If you're a refiner,
get an executor to complete
your detail work. If you're an
advancer, get a creator to come up with ideas for you. If
you're an executor, get a refiner to check the system for
you. No matter what your strengths, trade off the work
you're weak in to someone who was born to excel at it.

But if your strengths are very different from the other
person's strengths, you might need someone in between
to interpret for you. Put the right people in between.

Be careful about who works together and who doesn't.

CHAPTER 47

LEADERSHIP
YOU KNOW IT'S THERE WHEN NO ONE PUTS
CRAP LIKE THIS ON THE WALLS

I'VE BEEN DIAGNOSED WITH THE NUMBER-THREE CAUSE OF DEATH: NATURAL CAUSES

BY ALLEN FAHDEN

Only heart disease and cancer kill more people than natural causes. Look it up. That's why I giggle when motivational speakers tell you what disease they recovered from.

"That's nothing," I reply. "How would you like to die of a disease mostly called 'other?'"

Leadership. Team. Success. I also find motivational posters laughable. If a creator like me hates something, ridicule and parodies can be a side effect. That's why in 1995 I created the very first demotivational posters: Suckcess.

"Fahden, you idiot," one of my advancer friends said. (My friends often start their sentences that way.) "Give me those." He sent them to a major greeting card company. Even though they turned down 1,000 ideas a week, they sent us back a five-year contract.

To a creator, it's enough to have the idea and then brag about it. To an advancer, there is no satisfaction without action. Start by getting to know as many advancers as you can today. I'm trying to collect the whole set.

To an advancer, there is no satisfaction without action.

GIVE UP
DOING THIS

Believing that the people
you need to know are the
ones with money or other
symbols of success.

DO THIS INSTEAD

Start collecting people for your
team based on their core natures
so you can always hand off your
idea to someone who can move it
ahead or help you bulletproof it.

*Befriend as many advancers as you can. They
will set priorities and launch your best ideas.
Without the advancers, the great ideas die.*

CHAPTER 48

PASSION
THIS YEAR RE-IGNITE YOUR ZEST FOR APATHY

WHAT MICHAEL JORDAN FAILING AT BASEBALL TAUGHT ME ABOUT PASSION

BY MIKE VEECK

My dad, Bill Veeck, made baseball history with his unprecedented, one-at-bat-only hiring of Eddie Gaedel, a 3-foot 7-inch midget with a tiny strike zone. Hunched over in his batting stance, Eddie's strike zone was about four inches. The idea was for Eddie to walk in four pitches, which he easily did. The midget at bat became my dad's best-known baseball stunt and landed him in the Baseball Hall of Fame.

If Eddie had every baseball owner's dream strike zone, Michael Jordan's strike zone was a nightmare. Michael Jordan made baseball history by ending his retirement from what was arguably one of the most stunning, accomplished basketball careers to become a minor-league baseball player. At 6-foot 6-inches tall, Jordan was a right fielder with a huge strike zone. In baseball, they send you to cover right field when you are the worst player on the team.

How could perhaps the greatest NBA player of all time fail at minor-league baseball? It wasn't lack of passion. Jordan loved baseball just as much as hoops. So then, what made him bat only .211, strike out 114 times and make 11 errors in right field in lowly, Class AA, minor-league ball?
He was simply not suited to the game.

Passion for a subject alone isn't enough. Focus on strengths you apply to the content you're passionate about.

317

GIVE UP DOING THIS

Focusing only on what you're passionate about to help you choose the right career. Passion for the subject matter isn't enough.

DO THIS INSTEAD

Focus equally on what strengths you apply to the content that you're passionate about. That's what makes your day.

Work SRP: Let your Strength determine your Role
and then apply it to content that arouses your Passion.
That makes you a starring role performer.

CHAPTER 49

DISCOVERY

THEY FINALLY CALLED YOUR REFERENCES—
REPORT TO HUMAN RESOURCES

You're Miscast, Just Like These Idiots

BY ALLEN FAHDEN

Imagine how defeated these "idiots" must have felt when they stumbled in their lives, trying to find their way.

Walt Disney was fired by a newspaper editor, who told him he didn't have any creative ideas.

Albert Einstein couldn't talk until he was four years old and couldn't read until age seven.

Oprah Winfrey was terminated from her reporter's job because she was "unfit for TV."

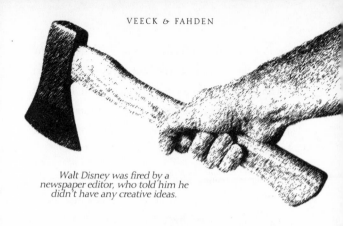

Walt Disney was fired by a newspaper editor, who told him he didn't have any creative ideas.

Think about your career. It's not just the content you need to be passionate about. It's the part of yourself that you apply to that content. To sustain you, this must be come from your strengths.

EXAMPLES

- 🔲 High Passion: I love baseball.

- 🔲 Low Passion: I don't love banking.

- 🔲 High Strength: Creating ideas.

- 🔲 Low Strength: Doing details.

Put me in a bank creating ideas, and I will probably lose my zeal for the job after a few short months because it's not that important to me to sell another checking account. I actually worked as senior vice president in charge of creative for the ad agency that handled most of the interior advertising for the largest bank chains in the United States.

I am strong at creating ideas. I am not passionate about banks. Whenever we created an exciting new marketing campaign, I felt plagued by an empty sense that I really hadn't done anything to make the world a better place.

Put me in a baseball team doing details, and I'll struggle, because details rob me of my energy. I don't think in a linear way and I easily make mistakes as I hurry to get it over with.

Put me in a bank doing details, and watch my soul quickly shrivel up and die.

But put me in a baseball team creating ideas, and I jump out of bed every morning excited about my day.

GIVE UP DOING THIS

Accepting tasks in your weak work zone so you can "pay your dues" and "be a team player." You'll wind up paying a bigger price and letting the team down.

DO THIS INSTEAD

Work in your peak work zone instead. Do your best and then hand off the rest to the next strength. You'll both star as the highest of performers. How do you tell when it's your peak work? If it energizes you, not drains you. You must love it (affinity) and be able to knock it out of the park (ability).

Strength or passion? We need to have both. Be true to your core work nature and work on your passion. Love it. Nail it.

CHAPTER 50

SERENDIPITY
THERE ARE ONLY 100 PEOPLE IN THE WORLD.
THE REST ARE EXTRAS

HOW TAKING CARE OF PEOPLE WHO COULDN'T DO ANYTHING FOR ME MADE MY DREAMS COME TRUE

BY MIKE VEECK

Whenever I'm at the Saint Paul Saints stadium, I always take tickets and greet the fans. I like to stay in contact with the people we're serving. One night I spotted Larry, a guy in a wheelchair, and offered to roll him up the ramp to our disabled area behind home plate. This became a habit night after night. I would see Larry and chat with him as I pushed his wheelchair to

My one big dream was to have Bob Dylan play at the St. Paul Saints stadium. Larry just smiled.

this special section. One night, Larry asked me about my dreams. I told him that my one big dream was to have Bob Dylan play at the St. Paul Saints stadium. Larry just smiled.

Four months later, I got a call from a guy in Los Angeles: "Bob wants to play your house," he said drily.

I was lost. "Who's Bob?" I asked, wondering how this guy had gotten my number.

"Dylan," he said as if I were a halfwit. "He wants to do a concert in your ballpark."

"Why?" I asked in shock, wondering if this was a prank call.

"'Cause Kegan told him he should," the man told me, as if this would explain everything.

"Who's Kegan?" I wondered out loud. This was getting more bizarre.

"Larry Kegan," the guy said slowly and loudly, not getting why I wasn't catching on. "He's in a wheelchair. He and Bob are old high-school pals."

Larry Kegan, a random fan I had gotten to know by trying to give personal customer service, made my unfulfilled fantasy come true.

GIVE UP
DOING THIS

Ignoring people you don't
think can do things for you.

DO THIS INSTEAD

Ask yourself: Who is it that I don't
make the time to talk with? If you
can only give to others when you
know there is something in it for
you, you will miss opportunities
you never saw coming.

Make friends with people who can't do something for you.
When you don't expect anything, you'll never be disappointed.

CHAPTER 51

MAKE THIS BOOK PAY: 180 MILLION TIMES OVER

YOU CAN BE AS NORMAL AS YOU WANT.
AND AT THE SAME TIME BE EXCEPTIONAL.

"NOBODY REALIZES THAT SOME PEOPLE *EXPEND* TREMENDOUS *ENERGY* MERELY TO BE *NORMAL*."

-ALBERT CAMUS

People always ask us, "What's my best takeaway from all this?" Do something! You can apply these methods and get fast results, no matter what stage of growth you're in.

SOME NORMAL COMPANIES THAT GOT EXCEPTIONAL RESULTS:

◘ A major energy company reported saving $1 million dollars a team using these techniques.

◘ A medium-sized marketing communications company used the Team Methods in this book to quadruple their business in one year. They went from seven million to $29 million in revenue with a 48% margin, in part just by being faster, and innovating more effectively.

◘ In just one hour, a small aerospace company solved a two-year-old impasse that was killing their growth.

◘ A large telecommunications company grew one division from $20 million to $60 million in revenue while all other divisions of the organization had no financial growth.

🞖 An internet startup leaped from zero to a $4 million valuation in a little over a year

GO TO THE NEXT STEP WITH
ALLEN, MIKE AND OUR
FUN IS GOOD TEAM.

🞖 Tools: Different and profound

🞖 Keynotes and Speeches: Funny and actionable

🞖 Training: Fun and engaging

🞖 Consulting: Insightful and effective

🞖 Coaching: Inspiring and sensible

LAUGH, LEARN, LEAP.

Get the one of a kind Fun Is Good approach to:

🞖 Innovation

🞖 Change

- Team

- Work Performance

- Employee Engagement

- Customer Engagement

- Culture

- Your Company's Brand

- Your Personal Brand

- The Power of Humor

Visit our website: funisgoodteam.com

ABOUT THE AUTHORS

MIKE VEECK

Mike Veeck is a nationally renowned speaker, entrepreneur, college professor, marketing, promotions and advertising expert as well as an owner of six successful minor league baseball teams. His name is synonymous with fun and creativity and he continues to blaze new trails each year. Who else would train a pig to deliver baseballs to the umpire, hire mimes to perform instant replays or lock fans out of the stadium to set an all-time attendance record for fewest people at a game?

The Veeck family started in baseball nearly a century ago when Mike's grandfather was president of the Chicago Cubs. Mike's father Bill, a member of the Baseball Hall of Fame, was the owner of the St. Louis Browns, Cleveland Indians, Chicago White Sox and the then minor league Milwaukee Brewers. Bill Veeck is remembered for signing Larry Doby, the first African –American to play in the American League (1947) and for sending 3-foot, 6-inch Eddie Gaedel to bat in a major league game. Mike began his baseball career with the Chicago White Sox and has also worked for the Detroit Tigers, Florida Marlins and Tampa Bay Rays.

It is with the belief that anything is possible and fun is crucial to success that Mike runs his companies. His Saint Paul Saints have become a model organization and along with this culture of fun, it's their willingness to take creative risks, forge innovative partnerships and deliver outstanding customer care that proves to be the positive difference that leads to success. It's no surprise then that SNL alum and film guy Bill Murray (a co-owner and partner with Mike in a number of ventures) serves as Team Psychologist / Director of Fun. Murray is sometimes seen taking tickets, selling programs, coaching third base and giving noogies. Fans love the positive vibe, family feel and great customer service they get at Mike's ballparks! This business philosophy has garnered national attention, with Mike being featured on NBC Nightly News, 60 Minutes, HBO Real Sports with Bryant Gumbel, ESPN Sports Center, The Late Show with David Letterman and many other national media outlets.

With his teams practicing all this fun and passion in the workplace, providing great customer care, exceeding aggressive sales goals and gaining national attention for his creative promotions and partnerships, Mike decided to highlight his coworkers and tell these stories in his book – Fun Is Good! In response to the success of the book and organizations asking to learn more of this philosophy, Mike created the consulting company of the same name, Fun Is Good. He and his team lead entertaining seminars, training sessions and keynote speeches across the country. Mike is a highly sought after speaker, allow-ing him the privilege of working with many companies each year, including 3M, The NBA, Deluxe Corporation, General Mills and NASCAR, to name just a few.

Mike and his wife, Libby, reside in Mt. Pleasant, South Carolina. He is the father or two children, William "Night Train" and Rebecca.

ALLEN FAHDEN

Just on the strength and uniqueness of his ideas, Allen Fahden has gotten the attention of people in groups of up to 50 million.

His One-Book Book Store, *ReadDundant*, appeared in *People Magazine*, on ABC News, the BBC, National Public Radio and in major city newspapers. The store featured only Fahden's book in 13 different departments.

His promotion for the Portland Beavers, during the Enron scandal (Arthur Andersen Appreciation Night) got him on CNN and ESPN. "It costs $5 to get into the ball game, but we give you a receipt for $10 for tax purposes."

Fahden has worked with clients Paul McCartney on his food venture and Bill Murray and Mike Veeck on their professional baseball teams.

As a speaker he appeared for 20 of the top 100 companies in the world, ranging from Amazon.com to Coca-Cola, GE and Disney. Shell Oil reported that using Allen's techniques saved them a million dollars per team. Allen's systems gave Qwest a 38% sales increase and division sales grew from $20 million to $60 million over the next two years.

Allen's Team Dimensions Profile assessment that streamlines innovation has sold more than a million copies worldwide.

He has written several books, including chapters on strength-based work for the best-selling book *The One Minute Millionaire* by *Chicken Soup for the Soul* author Mark Victor Hanson.

Allen spoke at the first *Fortune* Magazine Innovation Forum alongside Warren Buffet and the CEOs of the top Fortune 500 corporations. He has trained and entertained audiences in the United States, Canada, Malaysia, Singapore, Germany, and Spain.

Clients include:

3M

Amazon

Disney

Procter&Gamble

Coca-Cola

Hewlett-Packard

Whirlpool

Paul McCartney

Maytag

GE

S.C. Johnson

Lockheed-Martin

USWest

The Associated Press

Novartis Pharmaceuticals

Tampa Bay Rays

Eastman-Kodak

Blue Cross/Blue Shield

JP Morgan Chase

GlaxoSmithKline

University of Minnesota

Deloitte Touche

United Health Care

American Advertising Federation

Direct Marketing Assoc.

Apple

Wells Fargo

Cargill

U.S. Bank

Gannett

Imation

Medtronic

Fortune Magazine

McDonald's

APPENDIX

THE S.P.E.E.D RELAY TEAM.

S is for solutions. Everyone generates Ideas.

P is for priorities. Advancers choose the best idea.

E is for errors. Refiners warn of
what can go wrong.

E is for edits. Creators solve the
problems that refiners raise.

D is for details. Executors prepare the
idea to insert into the system.